PENGUIN LIFE

GAMES PEOPLE PLAY

Dr Eric Berne (1910–1970) was a prominent psychiatrist and bestselling author. He grew up in Montreal, Canada, and received his MD degree from McGill University in 1935. He completed his psychiatry training in the United States and then entered the US Army as a psychiatrist.

After the war, Dr Berne moved to Carmel, California. He continued his work as a psychiatrist, but felt increasingly frustrated with the psychoanalytic approaches at the time. As a result, he began developing a new and revolutionary theory, which he called Transactional Analysis. In 1958 he published the paper 'Transactional Analysis: A New and Effective Method of Group Therapy' where he outlined this new approach.

After creating Transactional Analysis, Dr Berne continued to develop and apply this new methodology. This led him to publish *Games People Play* and to found the International Transactional Analysis Association. *Games People Play* was recognised as a classic by his fellow professionals, but also proved hugely popular with general readers. It spent more than two years on the *New York Times* bestseller list after it was first released in 1964, and it has now sold more than five million copies worldwide, in over ten languages.

Dr Berne led an active life and continued his psychotherapy and writing duties up until his death in 1970. He left a remarkable legacy, including the creation of Transactional Analysis, *Games People Play* and more than thirty other books and articles.

Find out more at www.ericberne.com.

ERIC BERNE

Games People Play

THE PSYCHOLOGY OF HUMAN
RELATIONSHIPS

PENGUIN LIFE

AN IMPRINT OF

PENGUIN BOOKS

PENGUIN LIFE

UK | USA | Canada | Ireland | Australia
India | New Zealand | South Africa

Penguin Life is part of the Penguin Random House group of companies
whose addresses can be found at global.penguinrandomhouse.com.

First published in the United States of America by Grove Press, Inc. 1964
First published in Great Britain by André Deutsch 1966
Published in Penguin Books 1967
Published in Penguin Life 2016
013

Printed in Italy by Grafica Veneta S.p.A.

A CIP catalogue record for this book is available from the British Library

ISBN: 978-0-241-25747-0

www.greenpenguin.co.uk

MIX
Paper from
responsible sources
FSC® C018179

Penguin Random House is committed to a
sustainable future for our business, our readers
and our planet. This book is made from Forest
Stewardship Council® certified paper.

To my patients and students
who taught me more and more and are still
teaching me about games and the meaning of life

Contents

CONTENTS

PART THREE

BEYOND GAMES

CONTENTS

Preface

THIS book is primarily designed to be a sequel to my book *Transactional Analysis in Psychotherapy*,[1] but has been planned so that it can be read and understood independently. The theory necessary for the analysis and clear understanding of games has been summarized in Part I. Part II contains descriptions of the individual games. Part III contains new clinical and theoretical material which, added to the old, makes it possible to understand to some extent what it means to be game-free. Those desiring further background are referred to the earlier volume. The reader of both will note that in addition to the theoretical advances, there have been some minor changes in terminology and viewpoint based on further thinking and reading and new clinical material.

The need for this book was indicated by interested requests from students and lecture audiences for lists of games, or for further elaboration of games mentioned briefly as examples in a general exposition of the principles of transactional analysis. Thanks are due in general to these students and audiences, and especially to the many patients who exposed to view, spotted or named new games; and in particular to Miss Barbara Rosenfeld for her many ideas about the art and meaning of listening; and to Mr Melvin Boyce, Mr Joseph Concannon, Dr Franklin Ernst, Dr Kenneth Everts, Dr Gordon Gritter, Mrs Frances Matson, and Dr Ray Poindexter, among others, for their independent discovery or confirmation of the significance of many games.

Mr Claude Steiner, formerly Research Director of the San Francisco Social Psychiatry Seminars and presently in the Department of Psychology at the University of Michigan deserves special mention on two counts. He conducted the first experiments which confirmed many of the theoretical points at issue here, and as a result of these experiments he helped considerably in clarifying the nature of autonomy and of intimacy. Thanks are also due to Miss Viola Litt, the Secretary-Treasurer of the Seminars, and to Mrs Mary N. Williams, my personal secretary, for their continued help, and to Anne Garrett for her assistance in reading the proof.

SEMANTICS

For conciseness, the games are described primarily from the male point of view unless they are clearly feminine. Thus the chief player is usually designated as 'he', but without prejudice, since the same situation, unless otherwise indicated, could as easily be outlined with 'she', *mutatis mutandis*. If the woman's role differs significantly from the man's, it is treated separately. The therapist is similarly without prejudice designated as 'he'. The vocabulary and viewpoint are primarily oriented toward the practising clinician, but members of other professions may find this book interesting or useful.

Transactional game analysis should be clearly distinguished from its growing sister science of mathematical game analysis, although a few of the terms used in the text, such as 'payoff', are now respectably mathematical. For a detailed review of the mathematical theory of games see *Games & Decisions*, by R. D. Luce and H. Raiffa.[2]

Carmel, California, May 1962

REFERENCES

1. Berne, E., *Transactional Analysis in Psychotherapy*, Evergreen, 1961.
2. Luce, R. D., and Raiffa, H., *Games & Decisions*, Chapman & Hall, 1957.

Introduction

THE theory of social intercourse, which has been outlined at some length in *Transactional Analysis*,[1] may be summarized as follows.

Spitz has found[2] that infants deprived of handling over a long period will tend at length to sink into an irreversible decline and are prone to succumb eventually to intercurrent disease. In effect, this means that what he calls emotional deprivation can have a fatal outcome. These observations give rise to the idea of *stimulus-hunger*, and indicate that the most favoured forms of stimuli are those provided by physical intimacy, a conclusion not hard to accept on the basis of everyday experience.

An allied phenomenon is seen in grown-ups subjected to sensory deprivation. Experimentally, such deprivation may call forth a transient psychosis, or at least give rise to temporary mental disturbances. In the past, social and sensory deprivation is noted to have had similar effects in individuals condemned to long periods of solitary imprisonment. Indeed, solitary confinement is one of the punishments most dreaded even by prisoners hardened to physical brutality,[3,4] and is now a notorious procedure for inducing political compliance. (Conversely, the best of the known weapons against political compliance is social organization.)[5]

On the biological side, it is probable that emotional and sensory deprivation tends to bring about or encourage organic changes. If the reticular activating system[6] of the brain stem is not sufficiently stimulated, degenerative changes in the nerve cells may follow, at least indirectly. This may be a secondary effect due to poor nutrition, but the poor nutrition itself may be a product of apathy, as in infants suffering from marasmus. Hence a biological chain may be postulated leading from emotional and sensory deprivation through apathy to degenerative changes and death. In this sense, stimulus-hunger has the same relationship to survival of the human organism as food-hunger.

Indeed, not only biologically but also psychologically and socially, stimulus-hunger in many ways parallels the hunger for food. Such terms as malnutrition, satiation, gourmet, gourmand, faddist, ascetic, culinary arts, and good cook are easily transferred from the field of nutrition to the field of sensation. Overstuffing has its parallel in overstimulation. In both spheres, under ordinary conditions where ample supplies are available and a diversified menu is possible, choices will be heavily influenced by an individual's idiosyncrasies. It is possible that some or many of these idiosyncrasies are constitutionally determined, but this is irrelevant to the problems at issue here.

The social psychiatrist's concern in the matter is with what happens after the infant is separated from his mother in the normal course of growth. What has been said so far may be summarized by the 'colloquialism':[7] 'If you are not stroked, your spinal cord will shrivel up.' Hence, after the period of close intimacy with the mother is over, the individual for the rest of his life is confronted with a dilemma upon whose horns his destiny and survival are continually being tossed. One horn is the social, psychological and biological forces which stand in the way of continued physical intimacy in the infant style; the other is his perpetual striving for its attainment. Under most conditions he will compromise. He learns to do with more subtle, even symbolic, forms of handling, until the merest nod of recognition may serve the purpose to some extent, although his original craving for physical contact may remain unabated.

This process of compromise may be called by various terms, such as sublimation; but whatever it is called, the result is a partial transformation of the infantile stimulus-hunger into something which may be termed *recognition-hunger*. As the complexities of compromise increase, each person becomes more and more individual in his quest for recognition, and it is these differentia which lend variety to social intercourse and which determine the individual's destiny. A movie actor may require hundreds of strokes each week from anonymous and undifferentiated admirers to keep his spinal cord from shrivelling, while a scientist may keep physically and mentally healthy on one stroke a year from a respected master.

'Stroking' may be used as a general term for intimate physical contact; in practice it may take various forms. Some people literally stroke an infant; others hug or pat it, while some people pinch it playfully or flip it with a fingertip. These all have their analogues in conversation, so that it seems one might predict how an individual would handle a baby by listening to him talk. By an extension of meaning, 'stroking' may be employed colloquially to denote any act implying recognition of another's presence. Hence a *stroke* may be used as the fundamental unit of social action. An exchange of strokes constitutes a *transaction*, which is the unit of social intercourse.

As far as the theory of games is concerned, the principle which emerges here is that any social intercourse whatever has a biological advantage over no intercourse at all. This has been experimentally demonstrated in the case of rats through some remarkable experiments by S. Levine[8] in which not only physical, mental and emotional development but also the biochemistry of the brain and even resistance to leukemia were favourably affected by handling. The significant feature of these experiments was that gentle handling and painful electric shocks were equally effective in promoting the health of the animals.

This validation of what has been said above encourages us to proceed with increased confidence to the next section.

2 · THE STRUCTURING OF TIME

Granted that handling of infants, and its symbolic equivalent in grown-ups, recognition, have a survival value. The question is, What next? In everyday terms, what can people do after they have exchanged greetings, whether the greeting consists of a collegiate 'Hi!' or an Oriental ritual lasting several hours? After stimulus-hunger and recognition hunger comes *structure-hunger*. The perennial problem of adolescents is: 'What do you say to her (him) then? And to many people besides adolescents, nothing is more uncomfortable than a social hiatus, a period of silent, unstructured time when no one present can think of anything more interesting to say than: 'Don't you think the walls are perpendicular tonight?' The eternal problem of the human being is how to structure his waking hours. In this existential sense, the function of all social living is to lend mutual assistance for this project.

The operational aspect of time-structuring may be called programming. It has three aspects: material, social and individual. The most common, convenient, comfortable, and utilitarian method of structuring time is by a project designed to deal with the material of external reality: what is commonly known as work. Such a project is technically called an *activity*; the term 'work' is unsuitable because a general theory of social psychiatry must recognize that social intercourse is also a form of work.

Material programming arises from the vicissitudes encountered in dealing with external reality; it is of interest here only insofar as activities offer a matrix for 'stroking', recognition, and other more complex forms of social intercourse. Material programming is not primarily a social problem; in essence it is based on data processing. The activity of building a boat relies on a long series of measurements and probability estimates, and any social exchange which occurs must be subordinated to these in order for the building to proceed.

Social programming results in traditional ritualistic or semi-ritualistic interchanges. The chief criterion for it is local acceptability, popularly called 'good manners'. Parents in all parts of the world teach their children manners, which means that they know the proper greeting, eating, emunctory, courting and mourning rituals, and also how to carry on topical conversations with appropriate strictures and reinforcements. The strictures and reinforcements constitute tact or diplomacy, some of which is universal and some local. Belching at meals or asking after another man's wife are each encouraged or forbidden by local ancestral tradition, and indeed there is a high degree of inverse correlation between these particular transactions. Usually in localities where people belch at meals, it is unwise to ask after the womenfolk; and in localities where people are asking after the womenfolk, it is unwise to belch at meals. Usually formal rituals precede semi-ritualistic topical conversations, and the latter may be distinguished by calling them *pastimes*.

As people become better acquainted, more and more *individual programming* creeps in, so that 'incidents' begin to occur. These incidents superficially appear to be adventitious, and may be so described by the parties concerned, but careful scrutiny reveals that they tend to follow definite patterns which are amenable to sorting and classification, and that the sequence is circumscribed by unspoken rules and regulations. These regulations remain latent as long as the amities or hostilities proceed according to Hoyle, but they become manifest if an illegal move is made, giving rise to a symbolic, verbal or legal cry of 'Foul!' Such sequences, which in contrast to pastimes are based more on individual than on social programming, may be called *games*. Family life and married life, as well as life in organizations of various kinds, may year after year be based on variations of the same game.

To say that the bulk of social activity consists of playing games does not necessarily mean that it is mostly 'fun' or that the parties are not seriously engaged in the relationship. On the one hand, 'playing' football and other athletic 'games' may not be fun at all, and the players may be intensely grim; and such games share with gambling and other forms of 'play' the potentiality for being very serious indeed, sometimes fatal. On the other hand, some authors for instance Huizinga,[9] include under 'play' such serious things as cannibal feasts. Hence calling such tragic behaviour as suicide, alcohol and drug addiction, criminality or schizophrenia 'playing games' is not irresponsible, facetious or barbaric. The essential characteristic of human play is not that the emotions are spurious, but that they are regulated. This is revealed when sanctions are imposed on an illegitimate emotional display. Play may be grimly serious, or even fatally serious, but the social sanctions are serious only if the rules are broken.

Pastimes and games are substitutes for the real living of real intimacy. Because of this they may be regarded as preliminary engagements rather than as unions, which is why they are characterized as poignant forms of play. Intimacy begins when individual (usually instinctual) programming becomes more intense, and both social patterning and ulterior restrictions and motives begin to give way. It is the only completely satisfying answer to stimulus-hunger, recognition-hunger and structure-hunger. Its prototype is the act of loving impregnation.

Structure-hunger has the same survival value as stimulus-hunger. Stimulus-hunger and recognition-hunger express the need to avoid sensory and emotional starvation, both of which lead to biological deterioration. Structure-hunger expresses the need to avoid boredom, and Kierkegaard[10] has pointed out the evils which result from unstructured time. If it persists for any length of time, boredom becomes synonymous with emotional starvation and can have the same consequences.

The solitary individual can structure time in two ways: activity and fantasy. An individual can remain solitary even in the presence of others, as every schoolteacher knows. When one is a member of a social aggregation of two or more people, there are several options for structuring time. In order of complexity, these are: (1) Rituals; (2) Pastimes; (3) Games; (4) Intimacy; and (5) Activity, which may form a matrix for any of the others. The goal of each member of the aggregation is to obtain as many satisfactions as possible from his transactions with other members. The more accessible he is, the more satisfactions he can obtain. Most of the programming of his social operations is automatic. Since some of the 'satisfactions' obtained under this programming, such as self-destructive ones, are difficult to recognize in the usual sense of the word 'satisfactions', it would be better to substitute some more non-committal term, such as 'gains' or 'advantages'.

The advantages of social contact revolve around somatic and psychic equilibrium. They are related to the following factors: (1) the relief of tension; (2) the avoidance of noxious situations; (3) the procurement of stroking; and (4) the maintenance of an established equilibrium. All these items have been investigated and discussed in great detail by physiologists, psychologists, and psychoanalysts. Translated into terms of social psychiatry, they may be stated as (1) the primary internal advantages; (2) the primary external advantages; (3) the secondary advantages; and (4) the existential advantages. The first three parallel the 'gains from illness' described by Freud: the internal paranosic gain, the external paranosic gain, and the epinosic gain, respectively.[11] Experience has shown that it is more useful and enlightening to investigate social transactions from the point of view of the advantages gained than to treat them as defensive operations. In the first place, the best defence is to engage in no transactions at all; in the second place, the concept of 'defences' covers only part of the first two classes of advantages, and the rest of them, together with the third and fourth classes, are lost to this point of view.

The most gratifying forms of social contact, whether or not they are embedded in a matrix of activity, are games and intimacy. Prolonged intimacy is rare, and even then it is primarily a private matter; significant social intercourse most commonly takes the form of games, and that is the subject which principally concerns us here. For further information about time-structuring, the author's book on group dynamics should be consulted.[12]

REFERENCES

1. Berne, E., *Transactional Analysis in Psychotherapy*, Evergreen, 1961.

2. Spitz, R., 'Hospitalism: Genesis of Psychiatric Conditions in Early Childhood', *Psychoanalytic Study of the Child*, 1: 53–74, 1945.

3. Belbenoit, Rene, *Dry Guillotine*, Cape, 1938.

4. Seaton, G. J., *Scars on my Passport*, Hutchinson, 1951.

5. Kinkead, E., *Why they Collaborated*, Longmans, 1960.

6. French, J. D., 'The Reticular Formation', *Scientific American*, 196: 54–60, May 1957.

7. The 'colloquialisms' used are those evolved in the course of time at the San Francisco Social Psychiatry Seminars.

8. Levine, S., 'Stimulation in Infancy', *Scientific American*, 202: 80–86, May 1960.

Levine, S., 'Infantile Experience and Resistance to Physiological Stress', *Science*, 126: 405, 30 August 1957.

9. Huizinga, J., *Homo Ludens*, Routledge, 1949.

10. Kierkegaard, S., *A Kierkegaard Anthology* (ed. R. Bretall), Princeton University Press, 1947, pp. 22ff.

11. Freud, S., 'General Remarks on Hysterical Attacks', Standard Edn, II, Hogarth Press, London, 1955.

Freud, S., 'Analysis of a Case of Hysteria', ibid., VI, 1953.

12. Berne, E., *The Structure and Dynamics of Organizations and Groups*, Pitman Medical, 1963.

PART ONE

ANALYSIS OF GAMES

1 · Structural Analysis

OBSERVATION of spontaneous social activity, most productively carried out in certain kinds of psychotherapy groups, reveals that from time to time people show noticeable changes in posture, viewpoint, voice, vocabulary, and other aspects of behaviour. These behavioural changes are often accompanied by shifts in feeling. In a given individual, a certain set of behaviour patterns corresponds to one state of mind, while another set is related to a different psychic attitude, often inconsistent with the first. These changes and differences give rise to the idea of *ego states*.

In technical language, an ego state may be described phenomenologically as a coherent system of feelings, and operationally as a set of coherent behaviour patterns. In more practical terms, it is a system of feelings accompanied by a related set of behaviour patterns. Each individual seems to have available a limited repertoire of such ego states, which are not roles but psychological realities. This repertoire can be sorted into the following categories: (1) ego states which resemble those of parental figures; (2) ego states which are autonomously directed towards objective appraisal of reality and (3) those which represent archaic relics, still-active ego states which were fixated in early childhood. Technically these are called, respectively, exteropsychic, neopsychic, and archaeopsychic ego states. Colloquially their exhibitions are called Parent, Adult and Child, and these simple terms serve for all but the most formal discussions.

The position is, then, that at any given moment each individual in a social aggregation will exhibit a Parental, Adult or Child ego state, and that individuals can shift with varying degrees of readiness from one ego state to another. These observations give rise to certain diagnostic statements. 'That is your Parent' means: 'You are now in the same state of mind as one of your parents (or a parental substitute) used to be, and you are responding as he would, with the same posture, gestures, vocabulary, feelings, etc.' 'That is your Adult' means: 'You have just made an autonomous, objective appraisal of the situation and are stating these thought-processes, or the problems you perceive, or the conclusions you have come to, in a non-prejudicial manner.' 'That is your Child' means: 'The manner and intent of your reaction is the same as it would have been when you were a very little boy or girl.'

The implications are:

1. That every individual has had parents (or substitute parents) and that he carries within him a set of ego states that reproduce the ego states of those parents (as he perceived them), and that these parental ego states can be activated under certain circumstances (exteropsychic functioning). Colloquially: 'Everyone carries his parents around inside of him.'

2. That every individual (including children, the mentally retarded and schizophrenics) is capable of objective data processing if the appropriate ego state can be activated (neopsychic functioning) Colloquially: 'Everyone has an Adult.'

3. That every individual was once younger than he is now, and that he carries within him fixated relics from earlier years which will be activated under certain circumstances (archaeopsychic functioning). Colloquially: 'Everyone carries a little boy or girl around inside of him.'

At this point it is appropriate to draw Figure 1A, which is called a *structural diagram*. This represents, from the present viewpoint, a diagram of the complete personality of any individual. It includes his Parental, Adult, and Child ego states. They are carefully segregated from each other, because they are so different and because they are so often quite inconsistent with each other. The distinctions may not be clear at first to an inexperienced observer, but soon become impressive and interesting to anyone who takes the trouble to learn structural diagnosis. It will be convenient henceforth to call actual people parents, adults or children, with no capital letters; Parent, Adult and Child, capitalized, will be used when ego states are referred to. Figure 1B represents a convenient, simplified form of the structural diagram.

Before we leave the subject of structural analysis, certain complications should be mentioned.

1. The word 'childish' is never used in structural analysis, since it has come to have strong connotations of undesirability, and of something to be stopped forthwith or got rid of. The term 'childlike' is used in describing the Child (an archaic ego state), since it is more biological and not prejudicial. Actually the Child is in

many ways the most valuable part of the personality, and can contribute to the individual's life exactly what an actual child can contribute to family life: charm, pleasure and creativity. If the Child in the individual is confused and unhealthy, then the consequences may be unfortunate, but something can and should be done about it.

2. The same applies to the words 'mature' and 'immature'. In this system there is no such thing as an 'immature person'. There are only people in whom the Child takes over inappropriately or

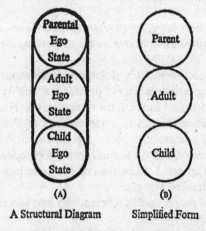

(A)   (B)

A Structural Diagram   Simplified Form

Figure 1. A Structural Diagram

unproductively, but all such people have a complete, well-structured Adult which only needs to be uncovered or activated. Conversely, so-called 'mature people' are people who are able to keep the Adult in control most of the time, but their Child will take over on occasion like anyone else's, often with disconcerting results.

3. It should be noted that the Parent is exhibited in two forms, direct and indirect: as an active ego state, and as an influence. When it is directly active, the person responds as his own father (or mother) actually responded ('Do as I do'). When it is an indirect influence, he responds the way they wanted him to respond ('Don't do as I do, do as I say'). In the first case he becomes one of them; in the second, he adapts himself to their requirements.

4. Thus the Child is also exhibited in two forms: the *adapted*

Child and the *natural* Child. The adapted Child is the one who modifies his behaviour under the Parental influence. He behaves as father (or mother) wanted him to behave: compliantly or precociously, for example. Or he adapts himself by withdrawing or whining. Thus the Parental influence is a cause, and the adapted Child an effect. The natural Child is a spontaneous expression: rebellion or creativity, for example. A confirmation of structural analysis is seen in the results of alcohol intoxication. Usually this decommissions the Parent first, so that the adapted Child is freed of the Parental influence, and is transformed by release into the natural Child.

It is seldom necessary, for effective game analysis, to go beyond what has been outlined above as far as personality structure is concerned.

Ego states are normal physiological phenomena. The human brain is the organ or organizer of psychic life, and its products are organized and stored in the form of ego states. There is already concrete evidence for this in some findings of Penfield and his associates.[1,2] There are other sorting systems at various levels, such as factual memory, but the natural form of experience itself is in shifting states of mind. Each type of ego state has its own vital value for the human organism.

In the Child reside intuition,[3] creativity and spontaneous drive and enjoyment.

The Adult is necessary for survival. It processes data and computes the probabilities which are essential for dealing effectively with the outside world. It also experiences its own kinds of setbacks and gratifications. Crossing a busy highway, for example, requires the processing of a complex series of velocity data; action is suspended until the computations indicate a high degree of probability for reaching the other side safely. The gratifications offered by successful computations of this type afford some of the joys of skiing, flying, sailing, and other mobile sports. Another task of the Adult is to regulate the activities of the Parent and the Child, and to mediate objectively between them.

The Parent has two main functions. First, it enables the individual to act effectively as the parent of actual children, thus promoting the survival of the human race. Its value in this respect is shown by the fact that in raising children, people orphaned in infancy seem to have a harder time than those from homes unbroken into adolescence. Secondly, it makes many responses automatic, which conserves a great deal of time and energy. Many things are done because 'That's the way it's done.' This frees the Adult from the necessity of making innumerable trivial decisions, so that it can devote itself to more important issues, leaving routine matters to the Parent.

Thus all three aspects of the personality have a high survival and living value, and it is only when one or the other of them disturbs the healthy balance that analysis and reorganization are indicated. Otherwise each of them, Parent, Adult, and Child, is entitled to equal respect and has its legitimate place in a full and productive life.

REFERENCES

1. Penfield, W., 'Memory Mechanisms', *Archives of Neurology & Psychiatry*, 67: 178–198, 1952.

2. Penfield, W., and Jasper, H., *Epilepsy and the Functional Anatomy of the Human Brain*, Churchill, 1954, Chapter 11.

3. Berne, E., 'The Psychodynamics of Intuition', *Psychiatric Quarterly*, 36: 294–300, 1962.

2 · Transactional Analysis

THE unit of social intercourse is called a transaction. If two or more people encounter each other in a social aggregation, sooner or later one of them will speak, or give some other indication of acknowledging the presence of the others. This is called the *transactional stimulus*. Another person will then say or do something which is in some way related to this stimulus, and that is called the *transactional response*. Simple transactional analysis is concerned with diagnosing which ego state implemented the transactional stimulus, and which one executed the transactional response. The simplest transactions are those in which both stimulus and response arise from the Adults of the parties concerned. The agent, estimating from the data before him that a scalpel is now the instrument of choice, holds out his hand. The respondent appraises this gesture correctly, estimates the forces and distances involved, and places the handle of the scalpel exactly where the surgeon expects it. Next in simplicity are Child-Parent transactions. The fevered child asks for a glass of water, and the nurturing mother brings it.

Both these transactions are *complementary*; that is, the response is appropriate and expected and follows the natural order of healthy human relationships. The first, which is classified as Complementary Transaction Type I, is represented in Figure 2A. The second, Complementary Transaction Type II, is shown in Figure 2B. It is evident, however, that transactions tend to proceed in chains, so that each response is in turn a stimulus. The first rule of communication is that communication will proceed smoothly as long as transactions are complementary; and its corollary is that as long as transactions are complementary, communication can, in principle, proceed indefinitely. These rules are independent of the nature and content of the transactions; they are based entirely on the direction of the vectors involved. As long as the transactions are complementary, it is irrelevant to the rule whether two people are engaging in critical gossip (Parent-Parent), solving a problem (Adult-Adult), or playing together (Child-Child or Parent-Child).

The converse rule is that communication is broken off when a *crossed transaction* occurs. The most common crossed transaction, and the one which causes and always has caused most of the social difficulties in the world, whether in marriage, love, friendship, or work, is represented in Figure 3A as Crossed Transaction Type I. This type of transaction is the principal concern of psychotherapists and is typified by the classical transference reaction of psychoanalysis. The stimulus is Adult-Adult: e.g., 'Maybe we should find out why you've been drinking more lately,' or, 'Do you know where my cuff links are?' The appropriate Adult-Adult response

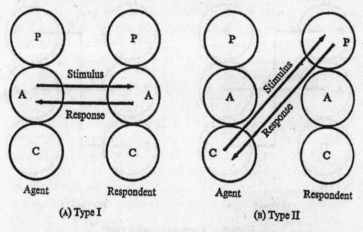

Figure 2. Complementary Transactions

in each case would be: 'Maybe we should. I'd certainly like to know!' or, 'On the desk.' If the respondent flares up, however, the responses will be something like 'You're always criticizing me, just like my father did,' or, 'You always blame me for everything.' These are both Child-Parent responses, and as the transactional diagram shows, the vectors cross. In such cases the Adult problems about drinking or cuff links must be suspended until the vectors can be realigned. This may take anywhere from several months in the drinking example to a few seconds in the case of the cuff links. Either the agent must become Parental as a complement to the respondent's suddenly activated Child, or the respondent's Adult must be reactivated as a complement to the agent's Adult. If the maid rebels during a discussion of dishwashing, the Adult-Adult conversation about dishes is finished; there can only ensue either a Child-Parent discourse, or a discussion of a different Adult subject, namely her continued employment.

The converse of Crossed Transaction Type I is illustrated in Figure 3B. This is the counter-transference reaction familiar to psychotherapists, in which the patient makes an objective, Adult observation, and the therapist crosses the vectors by responding like a parent talking to a child. This is Crossed Transaction Type

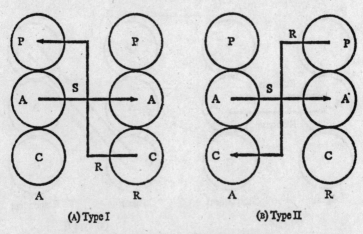

(A) Type I   (B) Type II

Figure 3. Crossed Transactions

II. In everyday life, 'Do you know where my cuff links are?' may elicit: 'Why don't you keep track of your own things? You're not a child any more.'

The *relationship diagram* in Figure 4, showing the nine possible vectors of social action between an agent and a respondent, has some interesting geometrical (topological) qualities. Complementary transactions between 'psychological equals' are represented by $(1–1)^2$, $(5–5)^2$ and $(9–9)^2$. There are three other complementary transactions: (2–4) (4–2), (3–7) (7–3) and (6–8) (8–6). All other combinations form crossed transactions, and in most cases these show up as crossings in the diagram: e.g., (3–7) (3–7), which results in two speechless people glaring at each other. If neither of them gives way, communication is finished and they must part. The most common solutions are for one to yield and take (7–3), which results in a game of 'Uproar'; or better, $(5-5)^2$, in which case they both burst out laughing or shake hands.

Simple complementary transactions most commonly occur in superficial working and social relationships, and these are easily disturbed by simple crossed transactions. In fact a superficial relationship may be defined as one which is confined to simple complementary transactions. Such relationships occur in activities,

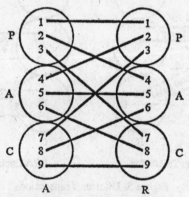

Figure 4. A Relationship Diagram

rituals and pastimes. More complex are *ulterior transactions* – those involving the activity of more than two ego states simultaneously – and this category is the basis for games. Salesmen are particularly adept at *angular transactions*, those involving three ego states. A crude but dramatic example of a sales game is illustrated in the following exchange:

Salesman: 'This one is better, but you can't afford it.'
Housewife: 'That's the one I'll take.'

The analysis of this transaction is shown in Figure 5A. The salesman, as Adult, states two objective facts: 'This one is better' and 'You can't afford it'. At the ostensible, or *social*, level these are directed to the Adult of the housewife, whose Adult reply would be: 'You are correct on both counts.' However, the ulterior, or *psychological*, vector is directed by the well-trained and experienced Adult of the salesman to the housewife's Child. The correctness of his judgement is demonstrated by the Child's reply, which says in effect: 'Regardless of the financial consequences, I'll show that arrogant fellow I'm as good as any of his customers.' At both levels the transaction is complementary, since her reply is accepted at face value as an Adult purchasing contract.

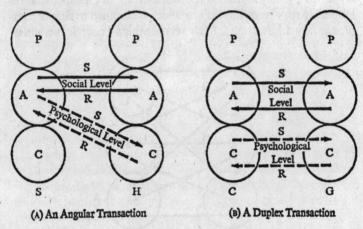

(A) An Angular Transaction   (B) A Duplex Transaction

Figure 5. Ulterior Transactions

A *duplex* ulterior transaction involves four ego states, and is commonly seen in flirtation games.

Cowboy: 'Come and see the barn.'
Visitor: 'I've loved barns ever since I was a little girl.'

As shown in Figure 5B, at the social level this is an Adult conversation about barns, and at the psychological level it is a Child conversation about sex play. On the surface the Adult seems to have the initiative, but as in most games, the outcome is determined by the Child, and the participants may be in for a surprise.

Transactions may be classified, then, as complementary or crossed, simple or ulterior, and ulterior transactions may be subdivided into angular and duplex types.

3 · Procedures and Rituals

TRANSACTIONS usually proceed in series. These series are not random, but are programmed. Programming may come from one of three sources: Parent, Adult or Child, or more generally, from society, material or idiosyncrasy. Since the needs of adaptation require that the Child be shielded by the Parent or Adult until each social situation has been tested, Child programming is most apt to occur in situations of privacy and intimacy, where preliminary testing has already been done.

The simplest forms of social activity are procedures and rituals. Some of these are universal and some local, but all of them have to be learned. A *procedure* is a series of simple complementary Adult transactions directed towards the manipulation of reality. Reality is defined as having two aspects: static and dynamic. *Static reality* comprises all the possible arrangements of matter in the universe. Arithmetic, for example, consists of statements about static reality. *Dynamic reality* may be defined as the potentialities for interaction of all the energy systems in the universe. Chemistry, for example, consists of statements about dynamic reality. Procedures are based on data processing and probability estimates concerning the *material* of reality, and reach their highest development in professional techniques. Piloting an airplane and removing an appendix are procedures. Psychotherapy is a procedure insofar as it is under the control of the therapist's Adult, and it is not a procedure insofar as his Parent or Child takes over the executive. The programming of a procedure is determined by the material, on the basis of estimates made by the agent's Adult.

Two variables are used in evaluating procedures. A procedure is said to be *efficient* when the agent makes the best possible use of the data and experience available to him, regardless of any deficiencies that may exist in his knowledge. If the Parent or the Child interferes with the Adult's data processing, the procedure becomes *contaminated* and will be less efficient. The *effectiveness* of a procedure is judged by the actual results. Thus efficiency is a psychological criterion and effectiveness is a material one. A native assistant medical officer on a tropical island became very adept at removing cataracts. He used what knowledge he had with a very high degree of efficiency, but since he knew less than the European medical officer, he was not quite as effective. The European began to drink heavily so that his efficiency dropped, but at first his effectiveness was not diminished. But when his hands became tremulous as the years went by, his assistant began to surpass him not only in efficiency, but also in effectiveness. It can be seen from this example that both of these variables are best evaluated by an expert in the procedures involved – efficiency by personal acquaintance with the agent, and effectiveness by surveying the actual results.

From the present viewpoint, a *ritual* is a stereotyped series of simple complementary transactions programmed by external social forces. An informal ritual, such as social leave-taking, may be subject to considerable local variations in details, although the basic form remains the same. A formal ritual, such as a Roman Catholic Mass, offers much less option. The form of a ritual is Parentally determined by tradition, but more recent 'parental' influences may have similar but less stable effects in trivial instances. Some formal rituals of special historical or anthropological interest have two phases: (1) a phase in which transactions are carried on under rigid Parental strictures (2) a phase of Parental licence, in which the Child is allowed more or less complete transactional freedom, resulting in an orgy.

Many formal rituals started off as heavily contaminated though fairly efficient procedures, but as time passed and circumstances changed, they lost all procedural validity while still retaining their usefulness as acts of faith. Transactionally they represent guilt-relieving or reward-seeking compliances with traditional Parental demands. They offer a safe, reassuring (apotropaic), and often enjoyable method of structuring time.

Of more significance as an introduction to game analysis are informal rituals, and among the most instructive are the American greeting rituals.

1A: 'Hi!' (Hello, good morning.)
1B: 'Hi!' (Hello, good morning.)
2A: 'Warm enough forya?' (How are you?)
2B: 'Sure is. Looks like rain, though.' (Fine. How are you?)
3A: 'Well, take cara yourself.' (Okay.)

3B: 'I'll be seeing you.'
4A: 'So long.'
4B: 'So long.'

It is apparent that this exchange is not intended to convey information. Indeed, if there is any information, it is wisely withheld. It might take Mr A fifteen minutes to say how he is, and Mr B, who is only the most casual acquaintance, has no intention of devoting that much time to listening to him. This series of transactions is quite adequately characterized by calling it an 'eight-stroke ritual'. If A and B were in a hurry, they might both be contented with a two-stroke exchange, Hi-Hi. If they were old-fashioned Oriental potentates, they might go through a two-hundred stroke ritual before settling down to business. Meanwhile, in the jargon of transactional analysis, A and B have improved each other's health slightly; for the moment, at least, 'their spinal cords won't shrivel up', and each is accordingly grateful.

This ritual is based on careful intuitive computations by both parties. At this stage of their acquaintance they figure that they owe each other exactly four strokes at each meeting, and not oftener than once a day. If they run into each other again shortly, say within the next half-hour, and have no new business to transact, they will pass by without any sign, or with only the slightest nod of recognition, or at most with a very perfunctory Hi-Hi. These computations hold not only for short intervals but over periods of several months. Let us now consider Mr C and Mr D, who pass each other about once a day, trade one stroke each – Hi-Hi – and go their ways. Mr C goes on a month's vacation. The day after he returns, he encounters Mr D as usual. If on this occasion Mr D merely says 'Hi!' and no more, Mr C will be offended, 'his spinal cord will shrivel slightly'. By his calculations, Mr D and he owe each other about thirty strokes. These can be compressed into a few transactions, if those transactions are emphatic enough. Mr D's side properly runs something like this (where each unit of 'intensity' or 'interest' is equivalent to a stroke):

1D: 'Hi!' (1 unit)
2D: 'Haven't seen you around lately.' (2 units)
3D: 'Oh, *have* you! Where did you go?' (5 units)
4D: '*Say, that's interesting.* How was it?' (7 units)

5D: 'Well, you're sure looking fine.' (4 units) 'Did your family go along?' (4 units)

6D: 'Well, glad to see you back.' (4 units)

7D: 'So long.' (1 unit)

This gives Mr D a total of 28 units. Both he and Mr C know that he will make up the missing units the following day, so the account is now, for all practical purposes, squared. Two days later they will be back at their two-stroke exchange, Hi-Hi. But now they 'know each other better', i.e., each knows the other is reliable, and this may be useful if they should meet 'socially'.

The inverse case is also worth considering, Mr E and Mr F have set up a two-stroke ritual, Hi-Hi. One day instead of passing on, Mr E stops and asks: 'How are you?' The conversation proceeds as follows:

1E: 'Hi!'

1F: 'Hi!'

2E: 'How are you?'

2F (*puzzled*): 'Fine. How are you?'

3E: 'Everything's great. Warm enough for you?'

3F: 'Yeah.' (*Cautiously.*) 'Looks like rain, though.'

4E: 'Nice to see you again.'

4F: 'Same here. Sorry, I've got to get to the library before it closes. So long.'

5E: 'So long.'

As Mr F hurries away, he thinks to himself: 'What's come over him all of a sudden? Is he selling insurance or something?' In transactional terms this reads: 'All he owes me is one stroke, why is he giving me five?'

An even simpler demonstration of the truly transactional, business-like nature of these simple rituals is the occasion when Mr G says 'Hi!' and Mr H passes on without replying. Mr G's reaction is 'What's the matter with him?' meaning: 'I gave him a stroke and he didn't give me one in return.' If Mr H keeps this up and extends it to other acquaintances, he is going to cause some talk in his community.

In borderline cases it is sometimes difficult to distinguish between a procedure and a ritual. The tendency is for the laymen to

call professional procedures rituals, while actually every transaction may be based on sound, even vital experience, but the layman does not have the background to appreciate that. Conversely,
there is a tendency for professionals to rationalize ritualistic elements that still cling to their procedures, and to dismiss sceptical
laymen on the ground that they are not equipped to understand.
And one of the ways in which entrenched professionals may resist
the introduction of sound new procedures is by laughing them off
as rituals. Hence the fate of Semmelweis and other innovators.

The essential and similar feature of both procedures and rituals
is that they are stereotyped. Once the first transaction has been
initiated, the whole series is predictable and follows a predeter-
mined course to a foreordained conclusion unless special conditions arise. The difference between them lies in the origin of the
predetermination: procedures are programmed by the Adult and
rituals are Parentally patterned.

Individuals who are not comfortable or adept with rituals sometimes evade them by substituting procedures. They can be found,
for example, among people who like to help the hostess with
preparing or serving food and drink at parties.

4 · Pastimes

PASTIMES occur in social and temporal matrices of varying degrees of complexity, and hence vary in complexity. However, if we use the transaction as the unit of social intercourse, we can dissect out of appropriate situations an entity which may be called a simple pastime. This may be defined as a series of semi-ritualistic, simple, complementary transactions arranged around a single field of material, whose primary object is to structure an interval of time. The beginning and end of the interval are typically signalled by procedures or rituals. The transactions are adaptively programmed so that each party will obtain the maximum gains or advantages during the interval. The better his adaptation, the more he will get out of it.

Pastimes are typically played at parties ('social gatherings') or during the waiting period before a formal group meeting begins; such waiting periods before a meeting 'begins' have the same structure and dynamics as 'parties'. Pastimes may take the form described as 'chit-chat' or they may become more serious, e.g., argumentative. A large cocktail party often functions as a kind of gallery for the exhibition of pastimes. In one corner of the room a few people are playing 'PTA', another corner is the forum for 'Psychiatry', a third is the theatre for 'Ever Been' or 'What Became', the fourth is engaged for 'General Motors', and the buffet is reserved for women who want to play 'Kitchen' or 'Wardrobe'. The proceedings at such a gathering may be almost identical, with a change of names here and there, with the proceedings at a dozen similar parties taking place simultaneously in the area. At another dozen in a different social stratum, a different assortment of pastimes is underway.

Pastimes may be classified in different ways. The external determinants are sociological (sex, age, marital status, cultural, racial or economic). 'General Motors' (comparing cars) and 'Who Won' (sports) are both 'Man Talk'. 'Grocery', 'Kitchen', and 'Wardrobe' are all 'Lady Talk' – or, as practised in the South Seas, 'Mary Talk'. 'Making Out' is adolescent, while the onset of middle age is marked by a shift to 'Balance Sheet'. Other species of this class, which are all variations of 'Small Talk', are: 'How To' (go about doing something), an easy filler for short airplane trips; 'How Much' (does it cost), a favourite in lower middle-class bars; 'Ever Been' (to some nostalgic place), a middle-class game for 'oldhands' such as salesmen; 'Do You Know' (so-and-so) for lonely ones; 'What Became' (of good old Joe), often played by economic successes and failures: 'Morning After' (what a hangover) and 'Martini' (I know a better way), typical of a certain kind of ambitious young person.

The structural-transactional classification is a more personal one. Thus 'PTA' may be played at three levels. At the Child-Child level it takes the form of 'How do You Deal with Recalcitrant Parents'; its Adult-Adult form, 'PTA' proper, is popular among well-read young mothers; with older people it tends to take the dogmatic Parent-Parent form of 'Juvenile Delinquency'. Some married couples play 'Tell Them Dear', in which the wife is Parental and the husband comes through like a precocious child. 'Look Ma No Hands' is similarly a Child-Parent pastime suitable for people of any age, sometimes diffidently adapted into 'Aw Shucks Fellows'.

Even more cogent is the psychological classification of pastimes. Both 'PTA' and 'Psychiatry', for example, may be played in either projective or introjective forms. The analysis of 'PTA Projective Type, is represented in Figure 6A, based on the following Parent-Parent paradigm:

A: 'There wouldn't be all this delinquency if it weren't for broken homes.'
B: 'It's not only that. Even in good homes nowadays the children aren't taught manners the way they used to be.'

'PTA', Introjective Type, runs along the following lines (Adult-Adult):

C: 'I just don't seem to have what it takes to be a mother.'
D: 'No matter how hard you try, they never grow up the way you want them to, so you have to keep wondering if you're doing the right thing and what mistakes you've made.'

'Psychiatry', Projective Type, takes the Adult-Adult form:

E: 'I think it's some unconscious oral frustration that makes him act that way.'

F: 'You seem to have your aggressions so well sublimated.'

Figure 6B represents 'Psychiatry', Introjective Type, another Adult-Adult pastime.

G: 'That painting symbolizes smearing to me.'

H: 'In my case, painting is trying to please my father.'

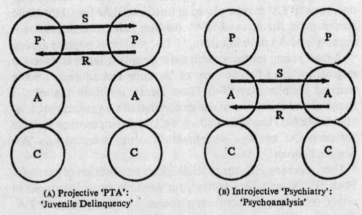

(A) Projective 'PTA':   (B) Introjective 'Psychiatry':
'Juvenile Delinquency'   'Psychoanalysis'

Figure 6. Pastimes

Besides structuring time and providing mutually acceptable stroking for the parties concerned, pastimes serve the additional function of being social-selection processes. While a pastime is in progress, the Child in each player is watchfully assessing the potentialities of the others involved. At the end of the party, each person will have selected certain players he would like to see more of, while others he will discard, regardless of how skilfully or pleasantly theyeach engaged in the pastime. The ones he selects are those who seem the most likely candidates for more complex relationships – that is, games. This sorting system, however well rationalized, is actually largely unconscious and intuitive.

In special cases the Adult overrides the Child in the selection process. This is most clearly illustrated by an insurance salesman who carefully learns to play social pastimes. While he is playing, his Adult listens for possible prospects and selects them from the players as people he would like to see more of. Their adeptness at games or congeniality is quite irrelevant to his process of selection, which is based, as in most cases, on peripheral factors – in this instance, financial readiness.

Pastimes, however, have a quite specific aspect of exclusiveness. For example, 'Man Talk' and 'Lady Talk' do not mix. People playing a hard hand of 'Ever Been' (there) will be annoyed by an intruder who wants to play 'How Much' (for avocados) or 'Morning After'. People playing Projective 'PTA' will resent the intrusion of Introjective 'PTA', athough usually not as intensely as the other way around.

Pastimes form the basis for the selection of acquaintances, and may lead to friendship. A party of women who drop in at each other's houses every morning for coffee to play 'Delinquent Husband' are likely to give a cool reception to a new neighbour who wants to play 'Sunny Side Up'. If they are saying how mean their husbands are, it is too disconcerting to have a newcomer declare that her husband is just marvellous, in fact perfect, and they will not keep her long. So at a cocktail party, if someone wants to move from one corner to another, he must either join in the pastime played in his new location or else successfully switch the whole proceeding into a new channel. A good hostess, of course, takes the situation in hand immediately and states the programme: 'We were just playing Projective "PTA". What do you think?' Or: 'Come now, you girls have been playing "Wardrobe" long enough Mr J here is a writer/politician/surgeon, and I'm sure he'd like to play "Look Ma No Hands". Wouldn't you, Mr J?'

Another important advantage obtained from pastimes is the confirmation of role and the stabilizing of position. A *role* is something like what Jung calls persona, except that it is less opportunistic and more deeply rooted in the individual's fantasies. Thus in Projective 'PTA' one player may take the role of tough Parent, another the role of righteous Parent, a third the role of indulgent Parent and a fourth the role of helpful Parent. All four experience and exhibit a Parental ego state, but each presents himself differently. The role of each one is confirmed if it prevails – that is, if it meets with no antagonism or is strengthened by any antagonism it meets or is approved by certain types of people with stroking.

The confirmation of his role stabilizes the individual's *position*, and this is called the *existential* advantage from the pastime. A position is a simple predicative statement which influences all of the individual's transactions; in the long run it determines his destiny and often that of his descendants as well. A position may be more or less absolute. Typical positions from which Projective 'PTA' can be played are: 'All children are bad!' 'All other children are bad!' 'All children are sad!' 'All children are persecuted!' These positions might give rise to the role of the tough, the righteous, the indulgent and the helpful Parent, respectively. Actually a position is primarily manifested by the mental *attitude* to which it gives rise, and it is with this attitude that the individual undertakes the transactions which constitute his role.

Positions are taken and become fixed surprisingly early, from the second or even the first year to the seventh year of life – in any case long before the individual is competent or experienced enough to make such a serious commitment. It is not difficult to deduce from an individual's position the kind of childhood he must have had. Unless something or somebody intervenes, he spends the rest of his life stabilizing his position and dealing with situations that threaten it: by avoiding them, warding off certain elements or manipulating them provocatively so that they are transformed from threats into justifications. One reason pastimes are so stereo-typed is that they serve such stereotyped purposes. But the gains they offer show why people play them so eagerly, and why they can be so pleasant if played with people who have constructive or benevolent positions to maintain.

A pastime is not always easy to distinguish from an activity, and combinations frequently occur. Many commonplace pastimes, such as 'General Motors', consist of what psychologists might call Multiple-Choice – Sentence-Completion exchanges.

A. 'I like a Ford/Chevrolet/Plymouth better than a Ford/Chevrolet/Plymouth because . . .'

B. 'Oh. Well, I'd rather have a Ford/Chevrolet/Plymouth than a Ford/Chevrolet/Plymouth because . . .'

It is apparent that there may actually be some useful information conveyed in such stereotypes.

A few other common pastimes may be mentioned. 'Me Too' is often a variant of 'Ain't It Awful'. 'Why Don't They' (do something about it) is a favourite among housewives who do not wish to be emancipated. 'Then We'll' is a Child-Child pastime. 'Let's Find' (something to do) is played by juvenile delinquents or mischievous grown-ups.

5 · Games

1 · DEFINITION

A GAME is an ongoing series of complementary ulterior transactions progressing to a well-defined, predictable outcome. Descriptively it is a recurring set of transactions, often repetitious, superficially plausible, with a concealed motivation; or, more colloquially, a series of moves with a snare, or 'gimmick'. Games are clearly differentiated from procedures, rituals, and pastimes by two chief characteristics: (1) their ulterior quality and (2) the payoff. Procedures may be successful, rituals effective, and pastimes profitable, but all of them are by definition candid; they may involve contest, but not conflict, and the ending may be sensational, but it is not dramatic. Every game, on the other hand, is basically dishonest, and the outcome has a dramatic, as distinct from merely exciting, quality.

It remains to distinguish games from the one remaining type of social action which so far has not been discussed. An *operation* is a simple transaction or set of transactions undertaken for a specific, stated purpose. If someone frankly asks for reassurance and gets it, that is an operation. If someone asks for reassurance, and after it is given turns it in some way to the disadvantage of the giver, that is a game. Superficially, then, a game looks like a set of operations, but after the payoff it becomes apparent that these 'operations' were really *manoeuvres*; not honest requests but moves in the game.

In the 'insurance game', for example, no matter what the agent appears to be doing in conversation, if he is a hard player he is really looking for or working on a prospect. What he is after, if he is worth his salt, is to 'make a killing'. The same applies to 'the real estate game', 'the pajama game' and similar occupations. Hence at a social gathering, while a salesman is engaged in pastimes, particularly variants of 'Balance Sheet', his congenial participation may conceal a series of skilful manoeuvres designed to elicit the kind of information he is professionally interested in. There are dozens of trade journals devoted to improving commercial manoeuvres, and which give accounts of outstanding players and games (interesting operators who make unusually big deals).

Transactionally speaking, these are merely variants of *Sports Illustrated, Chess World,* and other sports magazines.

As far as angular transactions are concerned – games which are consciously planned with professional precision under Adult control to yield the maximum gains – the big 'con games' which flourished in the early 1900s are hard to surpass for detailed practical planning and psychological virtuosity.[1]

What we are concerned with here, however, are the unconscious games played by innocent people engaged in duplex transactions of which they are not fully aware, and which form the most important aspect of social life all over the world. Because of their dynamic qualities, games are easy to distinguish from mere static *attitudes,* which arise from taking a position.

The use of the word 'game' should not be misleading. As explained in the introduction, it does not necessarily imply fun or even enjoyment. Many salesmen do not consider their work fun, as Arthur Miller made clear in his play, *The Death of a Salesman.* And there may be no lack of seriousness. Football games nowadays are taken very seriously, but no more so than such transactional games as 'Alcoholic' or 'Third-Degree Rapo'.

The same applies to the word 'play', as anyone who has 'played' hard poker or 'played' the stock market over a long period can testify. The possible seriousness of games and play, and the possibly serious results, are well known to anthropologists. The most complex game that ever existed, that of 'Courtier' as described so well by Stendhal in *The Charterhouse of Parma,* was deadly serious. The grimmest of all, of course, is 'War'.

2 · A TYPICAL GAME

The most common game played between spouses is colloquially called 'If It Weren't For You', and this will be used to illustrate the characteristics of games in general.

Mrs White complained that her husband severely restricted her social activities, so that she had never learned to dance. Due to changes in her attitude brought about by psychiatric treatment, her husband became less sure of himself and more indulgent. Mrs White was then free to enlarge the scope of her activities. She signed up for dancing classes, and then discovered to her despair that she had a morbid fear of dance floors and had to abandon this project.

This unfortunate adventure, along with similar ones, laid bare some important aspects of the structure of her marriage. Out of her many suitors she had picked a domineering man for a husband. She was then in a position to complain that she could do all sorts of things 'if it weren't for you'. Many of her women friends also had domineering husbands, and when they met for their morning coffee, they spent a good deal of time playing 'If It Weren't For Him'.

As it turned out, however, contrary to her complaints, her husband was performing a very real service for her by forbidding her to do something she was deeply afraid of, and by preventing her, in fact, from even becoming aware of her fears. This was one reason her Child had shrewdly chosen such a husband.

But there was more to it than that. His prohibitions and her complaints frequently led to quarrels, so that their sex life was seriously impaired. And because of his feelings of guilt, he frequently brought her gifts which might not otherwise have been forthcoming; certainly when he gave her more freedom, his gifts diminished in lavishness and frequency. She and her husband had little in common besides their household worries and the children, so that their quarrels stood out as important events; it was mainly on these occasions that they had anything but the most casual conversations. At any rate, her married life had proved one thing to her that she had always maintained: that all men were mean and tyrannical. As it turned out, this attitude was related to some daydreams of being sexually abused which had plagued her in earlier years.

There are various ways of describing this game in general terms. It is apparent that it belongs in the large field of *social dynamics*. The basic fact is that by marrying, Mr and Mrs White have an opportunity to communicate with each other, and such an opportunity may be called *social contact*. The fact that they use this opportunity makes their household a social aggregation, as contrasted with a New York subway train, for example, where people are in spatial contact but rarely avail themselves of the opportunity and so form a dis-social aggregation. The influence the Whites exert on each other's behaviour and responses constitutes *social action*. Various disciplines would investigate such social action from different points of view. Since we are here concerned with the personal histories and psychodynamics of the individuals involved, the present approach is one aspect of *social psychiatry*; some implicit judgement is passed on the 'healthiness' of the games studied. This is somewhat different from the more neutral and less committed attitudes of sociology and social psychology. Psychiatry reserves the right to say 'Just a moment!', which the other disciplines do not. Transactional analysis is a branch of social psychiatry, and game analysis is a special aspect of transactional analysis.

Practical game analysis deals with special cases as they appear in specific situations. Theoretical game analysis attempts to abstract and generalize the characteristics of various games, so that they can be recognized independently of their momentary verbal content and their cultural matrix. The theoretical analysis of 'If It Weren't For You', Marital Type, for example, should state the characteristics of that game in such a way that it can be recognized just as easily in a New Guinea jungle village as in a Manhattan penthouse, whether it is concerned with a nuptial party or with the financial problems of getting a fishing rod for the grandchildren; and regardless of how bluntly or subtly the moves are made, according to the permissible degrees of frankness between husband and wife. The *prevalence* of the game in a given society is a matter for sociology and anthropology. Game analysis, as a part of social psychiatry, is only interested in describing the game when it does occur, regardless of how often that may be. This distinction is not complete, but it is analogous to the distinction between public health and internal medicine; the first is interested in the prevalence of malaria, while the latter studies cases of malaria as they come up, in the jungle or in Manhattan.

At the present time the scheme given below has been found the most useful one for theoretical game analysis. No doubt it will be improved as further knowledge accumulates. The first requisite is to recognize that a certain sequence of manoeuvres meets the criteria of a game. As many samples as possible of the game are then collected. The significant features of the collection are isolated. Certain aspects emerge as essential. These are then classified under headings which are designed to be as meaningful and instructive as possible in the current state of knowledge. The analysis is undertaken from the point of view of the one who is 'it' – in this case, Mrs White.

Thesis. This is a general description of the game, including the immediate sequence of events (the social level) and information about their psychological background, evolution and significance (the psychological level). In the case of 'If It Weren't For You', Marital Type, the details already given will serve (pages 45–7). For the sake of brevity, this game will henceforth be referred to as IWFY.

Antithesis. The presumption that a certain sequence constitutes a game is tentative until it has been existentially validated. This validation is carried out by a refusal to play or by undercutting the payoff. The one who is 'it' will then make more intense efforts to continue the game. In the face of adamant refusal to play or a successful undercutting he will then lapse into a state called 'despair', which in some respects resembles a depression, but is different in significant ways. It is more acute and contains elements of frustration and bewilderment. It may be manifested, for example, by the onset of perplexed weeping. In a successful therapeutic situation this may soon be replaced by humorous laughter, implying an Adult realization: 'There I go again!' Thus despair is a concern of the Adult, while in depression it is the Child who has the executive power. Hopefulness, enthusiasm or a lively interest in one's surroundings is the opposite of depression; laughter is the opposite of despair. Hence the enjoyable quality of therapeutic game analysis. The antithesis to IWFY is permissiveness. As long as the husband is prohibitive, the game can proceed. If instead of saying 'Don't you dare!' he says 'Go ahead!' the underlying phobias are unmasked, and the wife can no longer turn on him, as demonstrated in Mrs White's case.

For clear understanding of a game, the antithesis should be known and its effectiveness demonstrated in practice.

Aim. This states simply the general purpose of the game. Sometimes there are alternatives. The aim of IWFY may be stated as either reassurance ('It's not that I'm afraid, it's that he won't let me') or vindication ('It's not that I'm not trying, it's that he holds me back'). The reassuring function is easier to clarify and is more in accord with the security needs of the wife; therefore IWFY is most simply regarded as having the aim of reassurance.

Roles. As previously noted, ego states are not roles but phenomena. Therefore ego states and roles have to be distinguished in a formal description. Games may be described as two-handed, three-handed, many-handed, etc., according to the number of roles offered. Sometimes the ego state of each player corresponds to his role, sometimes it does not.

I WFY is a two-handed game and calls for a restricted wife and a domineering husband. The wife may play her role either as a prudent Adult ('It's best that I do as he says') or as a petulant Child. The domineering husband may preserve an Adult ego state ('It's best that you do as I say') or slip into a Parental one ('You'd better do what I say').

Dynamics. There are alternatives in stating the psychodynamic driving forces behind each case of a game. It is usually possible, however, to pick out a single psychodynamic concept which usefully, aptly and meaningfully epitomizes the situation. Thus I WFY is best described as deriving from phobic sources.

Examples. Since the childhood origins of a game, or its infantile prototypes, are instructive to study, it is worth-while to search for such cognates in making a formal description. It happens that I WFY is just as frequently played by little children as by grown-ups, so the childhood version is the same as the later one, with the actual parent substituted for the restricting husband.

Transactional Paradigm. The transactional analysis of a typical situation is presented, giving both the social and psychological levels of a revealing ulterior transaction. In its most dramatic form I WFY at the social level is a Parent-Child game.

Mr White: 'You stay home and take care of the house.'
Mrs White: 'If it weren't for you, I could be out having fun.'

At the psychological level (the ulterior marriage contract) the relationship is Child-Child, and quite different.

Mr White: 'You must always be here when I get home. I'm terrified of desertion.'
Mrs White: 'I will be if you help me avoid phobic situations.'

The two levels are illustrated in Figure 7.

Moves. The moves of a game correspond roughly to the strokes in a ritual. As in any game, the players become increasingly adept with practice. Wasteful moves are eliminated, and more and more purpose is condensed into each move. 'Beautiful friendships' are often based on the fact that the players complement each other with great economy and satisfaction, so that there is a maximum yield with a minimum effort from the games they play with each other. Certain intermediate, precautionary or concessional moves can be elided, giving a high degree of elegance to the relationship.

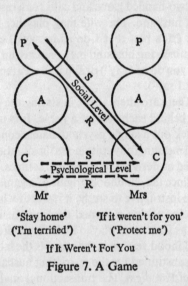

'Stay home'   'If it weren't for you'
('I'm terrified')   ('Protect me')

If It Weren't For You

Figure 7. A Game

The effort saved on defensive manoeuvres can be devoted to ornamental flourishes instead, to the delight of both parties and sometimes of the onlookers as well. The student observes that there is a minimum number of moves essential to the progress of the game, and these can be stated in the protocol. Individual players will embellish or multiply these basic moves according to their needs, talents or desires. The framework for IWFY is as follows

(1) Instruction-Compliance ('You stay home' – 'All right').

(2) Instruction-Protest ('You stay home again' – 'If it weren't for you').

Advantages. The general advantages of a game consist in its stabilizing (homeostatic) functions. Biological homeostasis is promoted by the stroking, and psychological stability is reinforced by the confirmation of position. As has already been noted, stroking may take various forms, so that the *biological advantage* of a game may be stated in tactile terms. Thus the husband's role in IWFY is reminiscent of a backhanded slap (quite different in effect from a palmar slap, which is a direct humiliation), and the wife's response is something like a petulant kick in the shins. Hence the biological gain from IWFY is derived from belligerence-petulance exchanges: a distressing but apparently effective way to maintain the health of nervous tissues.

Confirmation of the wife's position – 'All men are tyrants' – is the *existential advantage*. This position is a reaction to the need to surrender that is inherent in the phobias, a demonstration of the coherent structure which underlies all games. The expanded statement would be: 'If I went out alone in a crowd, I would be overcome by the temptation to surrender; at home I don't surrender: he forces me, which proves that all men are tyrants.' Hence this game is commonly played by women who suffer from feelings of unreality, which signifies their difficulty in keeping the Adult in charge in situations of strong temptation. The detailed elucidation of these mechanisms belongs to psychoanalysis rather than game analysis. In game analysis the end product is the chief concern.

Internal psychological advantage of a game is its direct effect on the psychic economy (libido). In IWFY the socially acceptable surrender to the husband's authority keeps the woman from experiencing neurotic fears. At the same time it satisfies masochistic needs, if they exist, using masochism not in the sense of self-abnegation but with its classical meaning of sexual excitement in situations of deprivation, humiliation or pain. That is, it excites her to be deprived and dominated.

External psychological advantage is the avoidance of the feared situation by playing the game. This is especially obvious in IWFY, where it is the outstanding motivation: by complying with the husband's strictures, the wife avoids the public situations which she fears.

Internal social advantage is designated by the name of the game as it is played in the individual's intimate circle. By her compliance, the wife gains the privilege of saying 'If it weren't for you'. This helps to structure the time she must spend with her husband; in the case of Mrs White, this need for structure was especially strong because of the lack of other common interests, especially before the arrival of their offspring and after the children were grown. In between, the game was played less intensively and less frequently, because the children performed their usual function of structuring time for their parents, and also provided an even more widely accepted version of I W F Y, the busy-housewife variation. The fact that young mothers in America often really are very busy does not change the analysis of this variation. Game analysis only attempts to answer this question without prejudice: given that a young woman is busy, how does she go about exploiting her busyness in order to get some compensation for it?

External social advantage is designated by the use made of the situation in outside social contacts. In the case of the game 'If It Weren't For You', which is what the wife says to her husband, there is a transformation into the pastime 'If It Weren't For Him' when she meets with her friends over morning coffee. Again, the influence of games in the selection of social companions is shown. The new neighbour who is invited for morning coffee is being invited to play 'If It Weren't For Him'. If she plays, well and good, she will soon be a bosom friend of the old-timers, other things being equal. If she refuses to play and insists on taking a charitable view of her husband, she will not last long. Her situation will be the same as if she kept refusing to drink at cocktail parties – in most circles, she would gradually be dropped from the guest lists.

This completes the analysis of the formal features of I W F Y. In order to clarify the procedure further, the analysis of 'Why Don't You – Yes But', which is the most common game played at social gatherings, committee meetings and psychotherapy groups the world over, should be consulted (page 101).

3 · THE GENESIS OF GAMES

From the present point of view, child rearing may be regarded as an educational process in which the child is taught what games to play and how to play them. He is also taught procedures, rituals and pastimes appropriate to his position in the local social situation, but these are less significant. His knowledge of and skill in procedures, rituals and pastimes determine what opportunities will be available to him, other things being equal; but his games determine the use he will make of those opportunities, and the outcomes of situations for which he is eligible. As elements of his script, or unconscious life-plan, his favoured games also determine his ultimate destiny (again with other things being equal): the payoffs on his marriage and career, and the circumstances surrounding his death.

While conscientious parents devote a great deal of attention to teaching their children procedures, rituals and pastimes appropriate to their stations in life, and with equal care select schools, colleges and churches where their teachings will be reinforced, they tend to overlook the question of games, which form the basic structure for the emotional dynamics of each family, and which the children learn through significant experiences in everyday living from their earliest months. Related questions have been discussed for thousands of years in a rather general, unsystematic fashion, and there has been some attempt at a more methodical approach in the modern orthopsychiatric literature; but without the concept of games there is little possibility of a consistent investigation. Theories of internal individual psychodynamics have so far not been able to solve satisfactorily the problems of human relationships. These are transactional situations which call for a theory of social dynamics that cannot be derived solely from consideration of individual motivations.

Since there are as yet few well-trained specialists in child psychology and child psychiatry who are also trained in game analysis, observations on the genesis of games are sparse. Fortunately, the following episode took place in the presence of a well-educated transactional analyst.

Tanjy, age seven, got a stomach-ache at the dinner table and asked to be excused for that reason. His parents suggested that he lie down for a while. His little brother Mike, age three, then said, 'I have a stomach-ache too,' evidently angling for the same consideration. The father looked at him for a few seconds and then replied, 'You don't want to play that game, do you?' Whereupon Mike burst out laughing and said, 'No!'

If this had been a household of food or bowel faddists, Mike would also have been packed off to bed by his alarmed parents. If he and they had repeated this performance several times, it might be anticipated that this game would have become part of Mike's character, as it so often does if the parents cooperate. Whenever he was jealous of a privilege granted to a competitor, he would plead illness in order to get some privileges himself. The ulterior trans-action would then consist of: (social level) 'I don't feel well' + (psychological level) 'You must grant me a privilege, too.' Mike, however, was saved from such a hypochondriacal career. Perhaps he will end up with a worse fate, but that is not the issue. The issue is that a game *in statu nascendi* was broken up right there by the father's question and by the boy's frank acknowledgement that what he proposed was a game.

This demonstrates clearly enough that games are quite deliber-ately initiated by young children. After they become fixed patterns of stimulus and response, their origins become lost in the mists of time and their ulterior nature becomes obscured by social fogs. Both can be brought into awareness only by appropriate proce-dures: the origin by some form of analytic therapy and the ulterior aspect by antithesis. Repeated clinical experience along these lines makes it clear that games are imitative in nature, and that they are initially set up by the Adult (neopsychic) aspect of the child's personality. If the Child ego state can be revived in the grown-up player, the psychological aptitude of this segment (the Adult aspect of the Child ego state) is so striking, and its skill in manipulating people so enviable, that it is colloquially called 'The Professor' (of Psychiatry). Hence in psychotherapy groups which concentrate on game analysis, one of the more sophisticated procedures is the search for the little 'Professor' in each patient, whose early adven-tures in setting up games between the ages of two and eight are listened to by everyone present with fascination and often, unless the games are tragic, with enjoyment and even hilarity, in which the patient himself may join with justifiable self-appreciation and smugness. Once he is able to do that, he is well on his way to relinquishing what may be an unfortunate behaviour pattern which he is much better off without.

Those are the reasons why in the formal description of a game an attempt is always made to describe the infantile or childhood prototype.

4 · THE FUNCTION OF GAMES

Because there is so little opportunity for intimacy in daily life, and because some forms of intimacy (especially if intense) are psychologically impossible for most people, the bulk of the time in serious social life is taken up with playing games. Hence games are both necessary and desirable, and the only problem at issue is whether the games played by an individual offer the best yield for him. In this connexion it should be remembered that the essential feature of a game is its culmination, or payoff. The principal function of the preliminary moves is to set up the situation for this payoff, but they are always designed to harvest the maximum permissible satisfaction at each step as a secondary product. Thus in 'Schlemiel' (making messes and then apologizing) the payoff, and the purpose of the game, is to obtain the forgiveness which is forced by the apology; the spillings and cigarette burns are only steps leading up to this, but each such trespass yields its own pleasure. The enjoyment derived from the spilling does not make spilling a game. The apology is the critical stimulus that leads to the denouement. Otherwise the spilling would simply be a destructive procedure, a delinquency perhaps enjoyable.

The game of 'Alcoholic' is similar: whatever the physiological origin, if any, of the need to drink, in terms of game analysis the imbibing is merely a move in a game which is carried on with the people in the environment. The drinking may bring its own kinds of pleasure, but it is not the essence of the game. This is demonstrated in the variant of 'Dry Alcoholic', which involves the same moves and leads to the same payoff as the regular game, but is played without any bottles (page 66).

Beyond their social function in structuring time satisfactorily, some games are urgently necessary for the maintenance of health in certain individuals. These people's psychic stability is so precarious, and their positions are so tenuously maintained, that to deprive them of their games may plunge them into irreversible despair and even psychosis. Such people will fight very hard against any antithetical moves. This is often observed in marital situations when the psychiatric improvement of one spouse (i.e., the abandonment of destructive games) leads to rapid deterioration in the other spouse, to whom the games were of paramount importance in maintaining equilibrium. Hence it is necessary to exercise prudence in game analysis.

Fortunately, the rewards of game-free intimacy, which is or should be the most perfect form of human living, are so great that even precariously balanced personalities can safely and joyfully relinquish their games if an appropriate partner can be found for the better relationship.

On a larger scale, games are integral and dynamic components of the unconscious life-plan, or script, of each individual; they serve to fill in the time while he waits for the final fulfilment, simultaneously advancing the action. Since the last act of a script characteristically calls for either a miracle or a catastrophe, depending on whether the script is constructive or destructive, the corresponding games are accordingly either constructive or destructive. In colloquial terms, an individual whose script is oriented towards 'waiting for Santa Claus' is likely to be pleasant to deal with in such games as 'Gee You're Wonderful, Mr Murgatroyd', while someone with a tragic script oriented towards 'waiting for *rigor mortis* to set in' may play such disagreeable games as 'Now I've Got You, You Son of a Bitch'.

It should be noted that colloquialisms such as those in the previous sentence are an integral part of game analysis, and are freely used in transactional psychotherapy groups and seminars. The expression 'waiting for *rigor mortis* to set in' originated in a dream of a patient, in which she decided to get certain things done 'before *rigor mortis* set in'. A patient in a sophisticated group pointed out what the therapist had overlooked: that in practice, waiting for Santa Claus and waiting for death are synonymous. Since colloquialisms are of decisive importance in game analysis, they will be discussed at length later on.

5 · THE CLASSIFICATION OF GAMES

Most of the variables used in analysing games and pastimes have already been mentioned, and any of them can be used in classifying games and pastimes systematically. Some of the more obvious classifications are based on the following factors:

1. Number of players: two-handed games (Frigid Woman), three-handed games (Let's You and Him Fight), five-handed games (Alcoholic) and many-handed games (Why Don't You – Yes But).

2. Currency used: words (Psychiatry), money (Debtor), parts of the body (Polysurgery).

3. Clinical types: hysterical (Rapo), obsessive-compulsive (Schlemiel), paranoid (Why Does This Have to Happen to Me), depressive (There I Go Again).

4. Zonal: oral (Alcoholic), anal (Schlemiel), phallic (Let's You and Him Fight).

5. Psychodynamic: counterphobic (If It Weren't for You), projective (PTA), introjective (Psychiatry).

6. Instinctual: masochistic (If It Weren't for You), sadistic (Schlemiel), fetishistic (Frigid Man).

In addition to the number of players, three other quantitative variables are often useful to consider:

1. Flexibility. Some games, such as Debtor and Polysurgery, can be played properly with only one kind of currency, while others, such as exhibitionistic games, are more flexible.

2. Tenacity. Some people give up their games easily, others are persistent.

3. Intensity. Some people play their games in a relaxed way, others are more tense and aggressive. Games so played are known as easy and hard games, respectively.

These three variables converge to make games gentle or violent. In mentally disturbed people, there is often a noticeable progression in this respect, so that one can speak of stages. A paranoid schizophrenic may initially play a flexible, loose, easy game of first-stage 'Ain't It Awful' and progress to an inflexible, tenacious, hard third stage. The stages in a game are distinguished as follows:

(a) A First-Degree Game is one which is socially acceptable in the agent's circle.

(b) A Second-Degree Game is one from which no permanent irremediable damage arises, but which the players would rather conceal from the public.

(c) A Third-Degree Game is one which is played for keeps, and which ends in the surgery, the courtroom or the morgue.

Games can also be classified according to any of the other specific factors discussed in the analysis of IWFY: the aims, the roles, the most obvious advantages. The most likely candidate for a systematic, scientific classification is probably one based on the existential position; but since knowledge of this factor is not yet sufficiently advanced, such a classification will have to be postponed. Failing that, the most practical classification at present is probably a sociological one. That is what will be used in the next section.

NOTES

Due credit should be given to Stephen Potter for his perceptive, humorous discussions of manoeuvres, or 'ploys', in everyday social situations,[2] and to G. H. Mead for his pioneering study of the role of games in social living.[3] Those games that lead to psychiatric disabilities have been systematically studied at the San Francisco Social Psychiatry Seminars since 1958, and this sector of game analysis has recently been approached by T. Szasz.[4] For the role of games in the group process, the present writer's book on group dynamics should be consulted.[5]

REFERENCES

1. Maurer, D. W., *The Big Con*, The Bobbs-Merrill Co., New York, 1940.
2. Potter, S., *Theory and Practice of Gamesmanship*, Rupert Hart-Davis, 1947.
3. Mead, G. H., *Mind, Self and Society*, Cambridge University Press, 1935.
4. Szasz, T., *The Myth of Mental Illness*, Secker & Warburg, 1961.
5. Berne, E., *The Structure and Dynamics of Organizations and Groups*, Pitman Medical, 1963.

PART TWO

A THESAURUS OF GAMES

Introduction

THIS collection is complete to date (1962), but new games are continually being discovered. Sometimes what appears to be another example of a known game turns out, on more careful study, to be an entirely new one, and a game which appears to be new often turns out to be a variation of a known one. The individual items of the analyses are also subject to change as new knowledge accumulates; for example, where there are several possible choices in describing dynamics, the statement given may turn out later not to have been the most cogent one. Both the list of games and the items given in the analyses, however, are adequate for clinical work.

Some of the games are discussed and analysed *in extenso*. Others, which require more investigation, or are uncommon, or whose significance is fairly obvious, are only briefly mentioned. The one who is 'it' is generally referred to as the 'agent', or is given the name of 'White', while the other party is called 'Black'.

The games are classified into families according to the situations in which they most commonly occur: Life Games, Marital Games, Party Games, Sexual Games and Underworld Games; then comes a section for professionals on Consulting Room Games, and finally, some examples of Good Games.

1 · NOTATION

The following notation will be used in the analytic protocols.

Title: if the game has a long name, a convenient abbreviation is used in the text. Where a game or its variations has more than one name, a cross reference will be found in the Index of Games. In oral reports it is preferable to use the full name of the game rather than its abbreviation or acronym.

Thesis: this is restated as cogently as possible.

Aim: this gives the most meaningful choice, based on the writer's experience.

Roles: the role of the one who is 'it', and from whose point of view the game is discussed, is given first, in italics.

Dynamics: as with aim.

Examples: (1) this gives an illustration of the game as played in childhood, the most easily recognizable pertinent prototype. (2) an illustration from adult life.

Paradigm: this illustrates as briefly as possible the critical trans-action or transactions at the social and psychological levels.

Moves: this gives the minimum number of transactional stimuli and transactional responses as found in practice. These may be expanded, diluted or ornamented to an unlimited extent in different situations.

Advantages: (1) Internal Psychological – this attempts to state how the game contributes to internal psychic stability. (2) External Psychological – this attempts to state what anxiety-arousing situations or intimacies are being avoided. (3) Internal Social – this gives the characteristic phrase used in the game as played with intimates. (4) External Social – this gives the key phrase used in the derivative game or pastime played in less intimate circles. (5) Biological – this attempts to characterize the kind of stroking which the game offers to the parties involved. (6) Existential – this states the position from which the game is typically played.

Relatives: this gives the names of complementary, allied and antithetical games.

An adequate understanding of a game can only be obtained in the psychotherapeutic situation. People who play destructive games will come to the therapist far more frequently than people who play constructive ones. Therefore most of the games which are well understood are basically destructive, but the reader should remember that there are constructive ones played by more fortunate people. And to prevent the idea of games from becoming vulgarized, as so many psychiatric terms are, it should be empha-sized once more that it is a very precise idea: games should be clearly distinguished, by the criteria given previously, from pro-cedures, rituals, pastimes, operations, manoeuvres and the atti-tudes which arise from various positions. A game is played from a position, but a position or its corresponding attitude is not a game.

2 · COLLOQUIALISMS

Many colloquialisms used here were supplied by patients. All of them, if used with due regard to timing and sensibilities, are appreciated, understood and enjoyed by the players. If some of them seem disrespectful, the irony is directed against the games and not against the people who play them. The first requirement for colloquialisms is aptness, and if they often sound amusing, that is precisely because they hit the nail on the head. As I have tried to show elsewhere in discussing colloquial epithets, a whole page of learned polysyllables may not convey as much as the statement that a certain woman is a bitch, or that a certain man is a jerk.[1] Psychological truths may be stated for academic purposes in scientific language, but the effective recognition of emotional strivings in practice may require a different approach. So we prefer playing 'Ain't It Awful' to 'verbalizing projected anal aggression'. The former not only has a more dynamic meaning and impact, but it is actually more precise. And sometimes people get better faster in bright rooms than they do in drab ones.

REFERENCE

1. Berne, E., 'Intuition IV: Primal Images & Primal Judgments', *Psychiatric Quarterly*, 29: 634–658, 1955.

6 · Life Games

ALL games have an important and probably decisive influence on the destinies of the players under ordinary social conditions; but some offer more opportunities than others for life-long careers and are more likely to involve relatively innocent bystanders. This group may be conveniently called Life Games. It includes 'Alcoholic', 'Debtor', 'Kick Me', 'Now I've Got You, You Son of a Bitch', 'See What You Made Me Do' and their principal variants. They merge on the one side with marital games, and on the other with those of the underworld.

1 · ALCOHOLIC

Thesis. In game analysis there is no such thing as alcoholism or 'an alcoholic', but there is a role called the Alcoholic in a certain type of game. If a biochemical or physiological abnormality is the prime mover in excessive drinking – and that is still open to some question – then its study belongs in the field of internal medicine. Game analysis is interested in something quite different – the kinds of social transactions that are related to such excesses. Hence the game 'Alcoholic'.

In its full flower this is a five-handed game, although the roles may be condensed so that it starts off and terminates as a two-handed one. The central role is that of the Alcoholic – the one who is 'it' – played by White. The chief supporting role is that of Persecutor, typically played by a member of the opposite sex, usually the spouse. The third role is that of Rescuer, usually played by someone of the same sex, often the good family doctor who is interested in the patient and also in drinking problems. In the classical situation the doctor successfully rescues the alcoholic from his habit. After White has not taken a drink for six months they congratulate each other. The following day White is found in the gutter.

The fourth role is that of the Patsy, or Dummy. In literature this is played by the delicatessen man who extends credit to White, gives him a sandwich on the cuff and perhaps a cup of coffee, without either persecuting him or trying to rescue him. In life this is more frequently played by White's mother, who gives him money and often sympathizes with him about the wife who does not understand him. In this aspect of the game, White is required to account in some plausible way for his need for money – by some project in which both pretend to believe, although they know what he is really going to spend most of the money for. Sometimes the Patsy slides over into another role, which is a helpful but not essential one: the Agitator, the 'good guy' who offers supplies without even being asked for them: 'Come have a drink with me (and you will go downhill faster).'

The ancillary professional in all drinking games is the bartender or liquor clerk. In the game 'Alcoholic' he plays the fifth role, the Connexion, the direct source of supply who also understands alcoholic talk, and who in a way is the most meaningful person in the life of any addict. The difference between the Connexion and the other players is the difference between professionals and amateurs in any game: the professional knows when to stop. At a certain point a good bartender refuses to serve the Alcoholic, who is then left without any supplies unless he can locate a more indulgent Connexion.

In the initial stages of 'Alcoholic', the wife may play all three supporting roles: at midnight the Patsy, undressing him, making him coffee and letting him beat up on her; in the morning the Persecutor, berating him for the evil of his ways; and in the evening the Rescuer, pleading with him to change them. In the later stages, due sometimes to organic deterioration, the Persecutor and the Rescuer can be dispensed with, but are tolerated if they are also willing to act as sources of supply. White will go to the Mission House and be rescued if he can get a free meal there; or he will stand for a scolding, amateur or professional, as long as he can get a handout afterwards.

Present experience indicates that the *payoff* in 'Alcoholic' (as is characteristic of games in general) comes from the aspect to which most investigators pay least attention. In the analysis of this game, drinking itself is merely an incidental pleasure having added advantages, the procedure leading up to the real culmination, which is the hangover. It is the same in the game of Schlemiel: the mess-making, which attracts the most attention, is merely a pleasure-giving way for White to lead up to the crux, which is obtaining forgiveness from Black.

For the Alcoholic the hangover is not as much the physical pain as the psychological torment. The two favourite pastimes of drinking people are 'Martini' (how many drinks and how they were mixed) and 'Morning After' (Let me tell you about *my* hangover). 'Martini' is played, for the most part, by social drinkers; many alcoholics prefer a hard round of psychological 'Morning After', and organizations such as Alcoholics Anonymous offer him an unlimited opportunity for this.

Whenever one patient visited his psychiatrist after a binge, he would call himself all sorts of names; the psychiatrist said nothing. Later, recounting these visits in a therapy group, White said with smug satisfaction that it was the psychiatrist who had called him all those names. The main conversational interest of many alcoholics in the therapeutic situation is not their drinking, which they apparently mention mostly in deference to their persecutors, but their subsequent suffering. The transactional object of the drinking, aside from the personal pleasures it brings, is to set up a situation where the Child can be severely scolded not only by the internal Parent but by any parental figures in the environment who are interested enough to oblige. Hence the therapy of this game should be concentrated not on the drinking but on the morning after, the self-indulgence in self-castigation. There is a type of heavy drinker, however, who does not have hangovers, and such people do not belong in the present category. ⟩

There is also a game 'Dry Alcoholic', in which White goes through the process of financial or social degradation without a bottle, making the same sequence of moves and requiring the same supporting cast. Here again, the morning after is the crux of the matter. Indeed, it is the similarity between 'Dry Alcoholic' and regular 'Alcoholic' which emphasizes that both are games; for example, the procedure for getting discharged from a job is the same in both. 'Addict' is similar to 'Alcoholic', but more sinister, more dramatic, more sensational and faster. In our society, at least, it leans more heavily on the readily available Persecutor, with Patsies and Rescuers being few and far between and the Connexion playing a much more central role.

There are a variety of organizations involved in 'Alcoholic', some of them national or even international in scope, others local. Many of them publish rules for the game. Nearly all of them explain how to play the role of Alcoholic: take a drink before breakfast, spend money allotted for other purposes, etc. They also explain the function of the Rescuer. Alcoholics Anonymous, for example, continues playing the actual game but concentrates on inducing the Alcoholic to take the role of Rescuer. Former Alcoholics are preferred because they know how the game goes, and hence are better qualified to play the supporting role than people who have never played before. Cases have been reported of a chapter of A.A. running out of Alcoholics to work on; whereupon the members resumed drinking, since there was no other way to continue the game in the absence of people to rescue.[1]

There are also organizations devoted to improving the lot of the other players. Some put pressure on the spouses to shift their roles from Persecutor to Rescuer. The one which seems to come closest to the theoretical ideal of treatment deals with teen-age offspring of alcoholics; these young people are encouraged to break away from the game itself, rather than merely shift their roles.

The psychological cure of an alcoholic also lies in getting him to stop playing the game altogether, rather than simply change from one role to another. In some cases this has been feasible, although it is a difficult task to find something else as interesting to the Alcoholic as continuing his game. Since he is classically afraid of intimacy, the substitute may have to be another game rather than a game-free relationship. Often so-called cured alcoholics are not very stimulating company socially, and possibly they feel a lack of excitement in their lives and are continually tempted to go back to their old ways. The criterion of a true 'game cure' is that the former Alcoholic should be able to drink socially without putting himself in jeopardy. The usual 'total abstinence' cure will not satisfy the game analyst.

It is apparent from the description of this game that there is a strong temptation for the Rescuer to play 'I'm Only Trying to Help You'; for the Persecutor to play 'Look What You've Done to Me'; and for the Patsy* to play 'Good Joe'. With the rise of rescue organizations which publicize the idea that alcoholism is a disease,

* In underworld slang 'patsy' once meant all right, or satisfactory, and later came to denote a 'pigeon'.

alcoholics have been taught to play 'Wooden Leg'. The law, which takes a special interest in such people, tends to encourage this nowadays. The emphasis has shifted from the Persecutor to the Rescuer, from 'I am a sinner' to 'What do you expect from a sick man?' (part of the trend in modern thinking away from religion and towards science). From an existential point of view the shift is questionable, and from a practical point of view it seems to have done little to diminish the sale of liquor to heavy drinkers. Nevertheless, Alcoholics Anonymous is still for most people the best initiation into the therapy of over-indulgence.

Antithesis. As is well known, 'Alcoholic' is usually played hard and is difficult to give up. In one case a female alcoholic in a therapy group participated very little until she thought she knew enough about the other members to go ahead with her game. She then asked them to tell her what they thought of her. Since she had behaved pleasantly enough, various members said nice things about her, but she protested: 'That's not what I want. I want to know what you really think.' She made it clear that she was seeking derogatory comments. The other women refused to persecute her, whereupon she went home and told her husband that if she took another drink, he must either divorce her or send her to a hospital. He promised to do this, and that evening she became intoxicated and he sent her to a sanitarium. Here the other members refused to play the persecutory roles White assigned to them; she was unable to tolerate this antithetical behaviour, in spite of everyone's efforts to reinforce whatever insight she had already obtained. At home she found someone who was willing to play the role she demanded.

In other cases, however, it appears possible to prepare the patient sufficiently so that the game can be given up, and to attempt a true social cure in which the therapist declines to play either Persecutor or Rescuer. It is equally untherapeutic for him to play the role of Patsy by allowing the patient to forgo his financial and punctuality obligations. The correct therapeutic procedure from a transactional point of view is, after careful preliminary ground-work, to take an Adult contractual position and refuse to play any of the roles, hoping that the patient will be able to tolerate not only abstinence from drinking but also from playing his game. If he cannot, he is best referred to a Rescuer.

Antithesis is particularly difficult, because the heavy drinker is highly regarded in most Western countries as a desirable object for censure, concern or generosity, and someone who refuses to play any of these roles tends to arouse public indignation. A rational approach may be even more alarming to the Rescuers than to the Alcoholic, sometimes with unfortunate consequences to the therapy. In one clinical situation a group of workers were seriously interested in the game 'Alcoholic' and were attempting to effect real cures by breaking up the game rather than merely rescuing the patients. As soon as this became apparent, they were frozen out by the lay committee which was backing the clinic, and none of them was ever again called on to assist in treating these patients.

Relatives. An interesting byplay in 'Alcoholic' is called 'Have One'. This was discovered by a perceptive student of industrial psychiatry. White and his wife (a non-drinking Persecutor) go on a picnic with Black and his wife (both Patsies). White says to the Blacks, 'Have one!' If they have one, this gives White licence to have four or five. The game is unmasked if the Blacks refuse. White, by the rules of drinking, is then entitled to be insulted, and he will find more compliant companions for his next picnic. What appears at the social level to be Adult generosity, is at the psychological level an act of insolence, whereby White's Child obtains Parental indulgence from Black by open bribery under the very nose of Mrs White, who is powerless to protest. Actually it is just because she will be 'powerless' to protest that Mrs White consents to the whole arrangement, since she is just as anxious for the game to continue, with herself in the role of Persecutor, as Mr White is with himself in the role of Alcoholic. Her recriminations against him in the morning after the picnic are easy to imagine. This variant can cause complications if White is Black's boss.

In general the Patsy is not as badly off as the name implies. Patsies are often lonely people who have a great deal to gain by being nice to Alcoholics. The delicatessen man who plays 'Good Joe' makes many acquaintances in this way, and he can get a good reputation in his own social circle not only as a generous person but also as a good storyteller.

One variant of 'Good Joe', incidentally, is to go around asking for advice about how best to help people. This is an example of a jolly and constructive game worth encouraging. Its inverse is Tough Guy, taking lessons in violence or asking for advice about how best to hurt people. Although the mayhem is never put into practice, the player has the privilege of associating with real tough guys who are playing for keeps, and can bask in their reflected glory. This is one species of what the French call *un fanfaron de vice*.

ANALYSIS

Thesis: How bad I've been; see if you can stop me.

Aim: Self-castigation.

Roles: Alcoholic, Persecutor, Rescuer, Patsy, Connexion.

Dynamics: Oral deprivation.

Examples: (1) See if you can catch me. The prototypes of this game are difficult to correlate because of its complexity. Children, however, particularly children of alcoholics, often go through many of the manoeuvres characteristic of the Alcoholic. 'See if you can stop me', which involves lying, hiding things, seeking derogatory comments, looking for helpful people, finding a bene-volent neighbour who will give free handouts, etc. Self-castigation is often postponed to later years. (2) The alcoholic and his circle.

Social Paradigm: Adult-Adult.

Adult: 'Tell me what you really think of me or help me stop drinking.'

Adult: 'I'll be frank with you.'

Psychological Paradigm: Parent-Child.

Child: 'See if you can stop me.'

Parent: 'You must stop drinking because . . .'

Moves: (1) Provocation – accusation or forgiveness. (2) Indul-gence – anger or disappointment.

Advantages: (1) Internal Psychological – (*a*) Drinking as a pro-cedure – rebellion, reassurance and satisfaction of craving. (*b*) 'Alcoholic' as a game – self-castigation (probable). (2) External Psychological – avoidance of sexual and other forms of intimacy. (3) Internal Social – See if you can stop me. (4) External Social – 'Morning After', 'Martini', and other pastimes. (5) Biological – alternating loving and angry exchanges. (6) Existential – Every-body wants to deprive me.

2 · DEBTOR

Thesis. 'Debtor' is more than a game. In America it tends to become a script, a plan for a whole lifetime, just as it does in some of the jungles of Africa and New Guinea.[2] There the relatives of a young man buy him a bride at an enormous price, putting him in their debt for years to come. Here the same custom prevails, at least in the more civilized sections of the country, except that the bride price becomes a house price, and if there is no stake from the relatives, this role is taken on by the bank.

Thus the young man in New Guinea with an old wrist watch dangling from his ear to ensure success, and the young man in America with a new wrist watch wrapped around his arm to ensure success, both feel that they have a 'purpose' in life. The big celebration, the wedding or housewarming, takes place not when the debt is discharged, but when it is undertaken. What is emphasized on TV, for example, is not the middle-aged man who has finally paid off his mortgage, but the young man who moves into his new home with his family, proudly waving the papers he has just signed and which will bind him for most of his productive years. After he has paid his debts – the mortgage, the college expenses for his children and his insurance – he is regarded as a problem, a 'senior citizen' for whom society must provide not only material comforts but a new 'purpose'. As in New Guinea, if he is very shrewd, he may become a big creditor instead of a big debtor, but this happens relatively rarely.

As this is written, a sow bug crawls across a desk. If he is turned over on his back, one can observe the tremendous struggle he goes through to get on his feet again. During this interval he has a 'purpose' in his life. When he succeeds, one can almost see the look of victory on his face. Off he goes, and one can imagine him telling his tale at the next meeting of sow bugs, looked up to by the younger generation as an insect who has made it. And yet mixed with his smugness is a little disappointment. Now that he has come out on top, life seems aimless. Maybe he will return in the hope of repeating his triumph. It might be worth marking his back with ink, so as to recognize him if he risks it. A courageous animal, the sow bug. No wonder he has survived for millions of years.

Most young Americans, however, take their mortgages very seriously only in times of stress. If they are depressed, or the economic situation is bad, their obligations keep them going and may prevent some of them from committing suicide. Most of the time they play a mild game of 'If It Weren't for the Debts', but otherwise enjoy themselves. Only a few make a career out of playing a hard game of 'Debtor'.

'Try and Collect' (TAC) is commonly played by young married couples, and illustrates how a game is set up so that the player 'wins' whichever way it goes. The Whites obtain all sorts of goods and services on credit, petty or luxurious, depending on their backgrounds and how they were taught to play by their parents or grandparents. If the creditor gives up after a few soft efforts to collect, then the Whites can enjoy their gains without penalty, and in this sense they win. If the creditor makes more strenuous attempts, then they enjoy the pleasures of the chase as well as the use of their purchases. The hard form of the game occurs if the creditor is determined to collect. In order to get his money he will have to resort to extreme measures. These usually have a coercive element – going to White's employers or driving up to his house in a noisy, garish truck labelled in big letters COLLECTION AGENCY.

At this point there is a switch. White now knows that he will probably have to pay. But because of the coercive element, made clear in most cases by the 'third letter' from the collector ('If you do not appear at our office within 48 hours . . .'), White feels peremptorily justified in getting angry; he now switches over to a variant of 'Now I've Got You, You Son of a Bitch'. In this case he wins by demonstrating that the creditor is greedy, ruthless and untrustworthy. The two most obvious advantages of this are (1) it strengthens White's existential position, which is a disguised form of 'All creditors are grasping', and (2) it offers a large external social gain, since he is now in a position to abuse the creditor openly to his friends without losing his own status as a 'Good Joe'. He may also exploit further internal social gain by confronting the creditor himself. In addition, it vindicates his taking advantage of the credit system: if that is the way creditors are, as he has now shown, why pay anybody?

'Creditor', in the form 'Try and Get Away With It' (TAG-AWI), is sometimes played by small landlords. TAC and TAG-AWI players readily recognize each other, and because of the prospective transactional advantages and the promised sport, they are secretly pleased and readily become involved with each other.

Regardless of who wins the money, each has improved the other's position for playing 'Why Does This Always Happen To Me?' after it is all over.

Money games can have very serious consequences. If these descriptions sound facetious, as they do to some people, it is not because they relate to trivia but because of the exposure of trivial motivations behind matters people are taught to take seriously.

Antithesis. The obvious antithesis of TAC is to request immediate payment in cash. But a good TAC player has methods for getting around that, which will work on any but the most hard-boiled creditors. The antithesis of TAGAWI is promptness and honesty. Since hard TAC and TAGAWI players are both professionals in every sense of the word, an amateur stands as much chance playing against them as he does playing against professional gamblers. While the amateur seldom wins, he can at least enjoy himself if he becomes involved in one of these games. Since both are by tradition played grimly, nothing is more disconcerting to the professionals than to have an amateur victim laugh at the outcome. In financial circles this is considered strictly Out. In the cases reported to this writer, laughing at a debtor when one encounters him on the street is just as bewildering, frustrating and disconcerting to him as playing anti-'Schlemiel' is to a Schlemiel.

3 · KICK ME

Thesis. This is played by men whose social manner is equivalent to wearing a sign that reads 'Please Don't Kick Me'. The temptation is almost irresistible, and when the natural result follows, White cries piteously, 'But the sign says "*don't* kick me".' Then he adds incredulously, 'Why does this always happen to me?' (WAHM). Clinically, the WAHM may be introjected and disguised in the 'Psychiatry' cliché: 'Whenever I'm under stress, I get all shook up.' One game element in WAHM comes from inverse pride: 'My misfortunes are better than yours.' This factor is often found in paranoids.

If the people in his environment are restrained from striking at him by kindheartedness, 'I'm Only Trying to Help You', social convention or organizational rules, his behaviour becomes more and more provocative until he transgresses the limits and forces them to oblige. These are men who are cast out, the jilted and the job losers.

The corresponding game among women is 'Threadbare'. Often genteel, they take pains to be shabby. They see to it that their earnings, for 'good' reasons, never rise much above the subsistence level. If they have a windfall, there are always enterprising young men who will help them get rid of it, giving them in return shares in a worthless business promotion or something equivalent. Colloquially, such a woman is called 'Mother's Friend', always ready to give judicious Parental advice and living vicariously on the experience of others. Their WAHM is a silent one, and only their demeanour of brave struggle suggests 'Why does this always happen to me?'

An interesting form of WAHM occurs in well-adapted people who reap increasing rewards and successes, often beyond their own expectations. Here the WAHM may lead to serious and constructive thinking, and to personal growth in the best sense, if it takes the form 'What did I really do to deserve this?'

4 · NOW I'VE GOT YOU, YOU SON OF A BITCH

Thesis. This can be seen in classic form in poker games. White gets an unbeatable hand, such as four aces. At this point, if he is a NIGYSOB player, he is more interested in the fact that Black is completely at his mercy than he is in good poker or making money.

White needed some plumbing fixtures installed, and he reviewed the costs very carefully with the plumber before giving him a go-ahead. The price was set, and it was agreed that there would be no extras. When the plumber submitted his bill, he included a few dollars extra for an unexpected valve that had to be installed – about four dollars on a four-hundred-dollar job. White became infuriated, called the plumber on the phone and demanded an explanation. The plumber would not back down. White wrote him a long letter criticizing his integrity and ethics and refused to pay the bill until the extra charge was withdrawn. The plumber finally gave in.

It soon became obvious that both White and the plumber were playing games. In the course of their negotiations, they had recognized each other's potentials. The plumber made his provocative move when he submitted his bill. Since White had the plumber's word, the plumber was clearly in the wrong. White now felt justified in venting almost unlimited rage against him. Instead of merely negotiating in a dignified way that befitted the Adult standards he set for himself, perhaps with a little innocent annoyance, White took the opportunity to make extensive criticisms of the plumber's whole way of living. On the surface their argument was Adult to Adult, a legitimate business dispute over a stated sum of money. At the psychological level it was Parent to Adult: White was exploiting his trivial but socially defensible objection (position) to vent the pent-up furies of many years on his cozening opponent, just as his mother might have done in a similar situation. He quickly recognized his underlying attitude (NIGYSOB) and realized how secretly delighted he had been at the plumber's provocation. He then recalled that ever since early childhood he had looked for similar injustices, received them with delight and exploited them with the same vigour. In many of the cases he recounted, he had forgotten the actual provocation, but remembered in great detail the course of the ensuing battle. The plumber, apparently, was playing some variation of 'Why Does This Always Happen to Me?' (WAHM).

NIGYSOB is a two-handed game which must be distinguished from 'Ain't It Awful' (AIA). In AIA the agent seeks injustices in order to complain about them to a third party, making a three-handed game: Aggressor, Victim, Confidant. AIA is played under the slogan 'Misery Loves Company'. The confidant is usually someone who also plays AIA. WAHM is three-handed, too, but here the agent is trying to establish his pre-eminence in misfortune and resents competition from other unfortunates. NIGYSOB is commercialized in a three-handed professional form as the 'badger game'. It may also be played as a two-handed marital game in more or less subtle forms.

Antithesis. The best antithesis is correct behaviour. The contractual structure of a relationship with a NIGYSOB player should be explicitly stated in detail at the first opportunity, and the rules strictly adhered to. In clinical practice, for example, the question of payment for missed appointments or cancellations must be settled clearly at once, and extra precautions must be taken to avoid mistakes in bookkeeping. If an unforeseen contretemps arises, the antithesis is to yield gracefully without dispute, until such time as the therapist is prepared to deal with the game. In everyday life, business dealings with NIGYSOB players are always calculated risks. The wife of such a person should be treated with polite correctness, and even the mildest flirtations, gallantries or slights should be avoided, especially if the husband himself seems to encourage them.

ANALYSIS

Thesis: Now I've got you, you son of a bitch.

Aim: Justification.

Roles: Victim, Aggressor.

Dynamics: Jealous rage.

Examples: (1) I caught you this time. (2) Jealous husband.

Social Paradigm: Adult-Adult.

Adult: 'See, you have done wrong.'

Adult: 'Now that you draw it to my attention, I guess I have.'

Psychological Paradigm: Parent-Child.

Parent: 'I've been watching you, hoping you'd make a slip.'

Child: 'You caught me this time.'

Parent: 'Yes, and I'm going to let you feel the full force of my fury.'

Moves: (1) Provocation – Accusation. (2) Defence – Accusation. (3) Defence – Punishment.

Advantages: (1) Internal Psychological – justification for rage. (2) External Psychological – avoids confrontation of own deficiencies. (3) Internal Social – NIGYSOB. (4) External Social – they're always out to get you. (5) Biological – belligerent exchanges, usually ipsisexual. (6) Existential – people can't be trusted.

5 · SEE WHAT YOU MADE ME DO

Thesis. In its classical form this is a marital game, and in fact is a 'three-star marriage buster', but it may also be played between parents and children and in working life.

(1) First-Degree SWYMD: White, feeling unsociable, becomes engrossed in some activity which tends to insulate him against people. Perhaps all he wants at the moment is to be left alone. An intruder, such as his wife or one of his children, comes either for

stroking or to ask him something like, 'Where can I find the long-nosed pliers?' This interruption 'causes' his chisel, paintbrush, typewriter or soldering iron to slip, whereupon he turns on the intruder in a rage and cries, 'See what you made me do.' As this is repeated through the years, his family tends more and more to leave him alone when he is engrossed. Of course it is not the intruder but his own irritation which 'causes' the slip, and he is only too happy when it occurs, since it gives him a lever for ejecting the visitor. Unfortunately this is a game which is only too easily learned by young children, so that it is easily passed on from generation to generation. The underlying satisfactions and advantages are more clearly demonstrated when it is played more seductively.

(2) Second-Degree SWYMD: If SWYMD is the basis for a way of life, rather than merely being used occasionally as a protective mechanism, White marries a woman who plays 'I'm Only Trying to Help You' or one of its relatives. It is then easy for him to defer decisions to her. Often this may be done in the guise of considerateness or gallantry. He may deferentially and courteously let her decide where to go for dinner or which movie to see. If things turn out well, he can enjoy them. If not, he can blame her by saying or implying: 'You Got Me Into This', a simple variation of SWYMD. Or he may throw the burden of decisions regarding the children's upbringing on her, while he acts as executive officer; if the children get upset, he can play a straight game of SWYMD. This lays the groundwork through the years for blaming mother if the children turn out badly; then SWYMD is not an end in itself, but merely offers passing satisfaction on the way to 'I Told You So' or 'See What You've Done Now'.

The professional player who pays his psychological way with SWYMD will use it also in his work. In occupational SWYMD the long-suffering look of resentment replaces words. The player 'democratically' or as part of 'good management' asks his assistants for suggestions. In this way he may attain an unassailable position for terrorizing his juniors. Any mistake he makes can be used against them by blaming them for it. Used against seniors (blaming them for one's mistakes), it becomes self-destructive and may lead to termination of employment or, in the army, to transfer to another unit. In that case it is a component of 'Why Does This

Always Happen To Me?' with resentful people, or of 'There I Go Again' with depressives – (both of the 'Kick Me' family).

(3) Third-Degree SWYMD: in a hard form SWYMD may be played by paranoids against people incautious enough to give them advice (see 'I'm Only Trying to Help You'). There it may be dangerous, and in rare cases even fatal.

'See What You Made Me Do' (SWYMD) and 'You Got Me into This' (UGMIT) complement each other nicely, so that the SWYMD-UGMIT combination is a classical basis for the cover game contract in many marriages. This contract is illustrated by the following sequence.

By mutual agreement Mrs White did the family bookkeeping and paid the bills out of the joint checking account because Mr White was 'poor at figures'. Every few months they would be notified of an overdraft, and Mr White would have to square it with the bank. When they looked for the source of the difficulty, it would turn out that Mrs White had made an expensive purchase without telling her husband. When this came to light, Mr White would furiously play his UGMIT, and she would tearfully accept his rebuke and promise it would not happen again. Everything would go smoothly for a while, and then a creditor's agent would suddenly appear to demand payment for a long-overdue bill. Mr White, not having heard of this bill, would question his wife about it. She would then play her SWYMD, saying that it was his fault. Since he had forbidden her to overdraw their account, the only way she could make ends meet was by leaving this large obligation unpaid and hiding the duns from him.

These games had been allowed to go on for ten years, on the basis that each occurrence would be the last, and that from then on it would be different – which it was, for a few months. In therapy Mr White very cleverly analysed this game without any assistance from the therapist, and also devised an effective remedy. By mutual agreement he and Mrs White put all charge accounts and their bank account in his name. Mrs White continued to do the book-keeping and make out the checks, but Mr White saw the bills first and controlled the outgoing payments. In this way neither duns nor overdrafts could get by him, and they now shared the budge-tary labour. Deprived of the satisfactions and advantages of SWYMD-UGMIT, the Whites were at first at a loss, and were then driven to find more open and constructive types of gratification from each other.

Antithesis. The antithesis to First-Degree SWYMD is to leave the player alone, and to Second-Degree SWYMD to throw the decision back on White. The First-Degree player may react by feeling forlorn, but seldom angry; the Second-Degree player may become sulky if he is forced to take the initiative, so that systematic anti-SWYMD leads to disagreeable consequences. The antithesis to Third-Degree SWYMD should be put into competent professional hands.

PARTIAL ANALYSIS

The aim of this game is vindication. Dynamically the mild form may be related to premature ejaculation, the hard form to rage based on 'castration' anxiety. It is easily acquired by children. The external psychological gain (avoidance of responsibility) is prominent, and the game is often precipitated by the threat of impending intimacy, since the 'justifiable' anger offers a good excuse for avoiding sexual relations. The existential position is, 'I am blameless'.

NOTE

Thanks are due to Dr Rodney Nurse and Mrs Frances Matson of the Center for Treatment and Education on Alcoholism in Oakland, California, and to Dr Kenneth Everts, Dr R. J. Starrels, Dr Robert Goulding and others with a special interest in this problem, for their continued efforts in the study of 'Alcoholic' as a game, and for their contribution to and criticism of the present discussion.

REFERENCES

1. Berne, E., *A Layman's Guide to Psychiatry & Psychoanalysis*, Simon & Schuster, New York, 1957, p. 191.

2. Mead, M., *Growing Up in New Guinea*, Morrow, New York, 1951.

7 · Marital Games

ALMOST any game can form the scaffolding for married life and family living, but some, such as 'If It Weren't for You', flourish better or, like 'Frigid Woman', are tolerated longer, under the legal force of contractual intimacy. Marital games, of course, can only be arbitrarily separated from sexual games, which are treated in a separate section. Those games which characteristically evolve into their most full-blown forms in the marital relationship include 'Corner', 'Courtroom', 'Frigid Woman' and 'Frigid Man', 'Harried', 'If It Weren't for You', 'Look How Hard I've Tried' and 'Sweetheart'.

1 · CORNER

Thesis. Corner illustrates more clearly than most games their manipulative aspect and their function as barriers to intimacy. Paradoxically, it consists of a disingenuous refusal to play the game of another.

1. Mrs White suggests to her husband that they go to a movie. Mr White agrees.

2a. Mrs White makes an 'unconscious' slip. She mentions quite naturally in the course of conversation that the house needs painting. This is an expensive project, and White has recently told her that their finances are strained; he requested her not to embarrass or annoy him by suggesting unusual expenditures, at least until the beginning of the new month. This is therefore an ill-chosen moment to bring up the condition of the house, and White responds rudely.

2b. Alternatively: White steers the conversation around to the house, making it difficult for Mrs White to resist the temptation to say that it needs painting. As in the previous case, White responds rudely.

3. Mrs White takes offence and says that if he is in one of his bad moods, she will not go to the movie with him, and he had best go by himself. He says if that is the way she feels about it, he will go alone.

4. White goes to the movie (or out with the boys), leaving Mrs White at home to nurse her injured feelings.

There are two possible gimmicks in this game:

A. Mrs White knows very well from past experience that she is not supposed to take his annoyance seriously. What he really wants is for her to show some appreciation of how hard he works to earn their living; then they could go off happily together. But she refuses to play, and he feels badly let down. He leaves filled with disappointment and resentment, while she stays at home looking abused, but with a secret feeling of triumph.

B. White knows very well from past experience that he is not supposed to take her pique seriously. What she really wants is to be honeyed out of it; then they would go off happily together. But he refuses to play, knowing that his refusal is dishonest: he knows she wants to be coaxed, but pretends he doesn't. He leaves the house, feeling cheerful and relieved, but looking wronged. She is left feeling disappointed and resentful.

In each of these cases the winner's position is, from a naïve standpoint, irreproachable; all he or she has done is take the other literally. This is clearer in (B), where White takes Mrs White's refusal to go at face value. They both know that this is cheating, but since she said it, she is cornered.

The most obvious gain here is the external psychological. Both of them find movies sexually stimulating, and it is more or less anticipated that after they return from the theatre, they will make love. Hence whichever one of them wants to avoid intimacy sets up the game in move (2a) or (2b). This is a particularly exasperating variety of 'Uproar' (see Chapter 9). The 'wronged' party can, of course, make a good case for not wanting to make love in a state of justifiable indignation, and the cornered spouse has no recourse.

Antithesis. This is simple for Mrs White. All she has to do is change her mind, take her husband by the arm, smile and go along with him (a shift from Child to Adult ego state). It is more difficult for Mr White, since she now has the initiative; but if he reviews the whole situation, he may be able to coax her into going along with him, either as a sulky Child who has been placated or, better, as an Adult.

'Corner' is found in a somewhat different form as a family game

involving the children, where it resembles the 'double-bind' described by Bateson and his associates.[1] Here the child is cornered,
so that whatever he does is wrong. According to the Bateson school
this may be an important etiological factor in schizophrenia. In
the present language, then, schizophrenia may be a child's antithesis to 'Corner'. Experience in treating adult schizophrenics
with game analysis bears this out – that is, if the family game of
'Corner' is analysed to demonstrate that the schizophrenic
behaviour was and is specifically undertaken to counter this
game, partial or total remission occurs in a properly prepared
patient.

An everyday form of 'Corner' which is played by the whole
family and is most likely to affect the character development of the
younger children occurs with meddlesome 'Parental' parents. The
little boy or girl is urged to be more helpful around the house, but
when he is, the parents find fault with what he does – a homely
example of 'damned if you do and damned if you don't'. This
'double-bind' may be called the Dilemma Type of 'Corner'.

'Corner' is sometimes found as an etiological factor in asth-
matic children.

> Little girl: 'Mummy, do you love me?'
> Mother: 'What is love?'

This answer leaves the child with no direct recourse. She wants
to talk about mother, and mother switches the subject to philo-
sophy, which the little girl is not equipped to handle. She begins
to breathe hard, mother is irritated, asthma sets in, mother apolo-
gizes and the 'Asthma Game' now runs its course. This 'Asthma'
type of 'Corner' remains to be studied further.

An elegant variant, which may be called the 'Russell-Whitehead
Type' of 'Corner', sometimes occurs in therapy groups.

> Black: 'Well, anyway, when we're silent nobody is playing
> games.'
> White: 'Silence itself may be a game.'
> Red: 'Nobody was playing games today.'
> White: 'But not playing games may itself be a game.'

The therapeutic antithesis is equally elegant. Logical paradoxes are forbidden. When White is deprived of this manoeuvre, his underlying anxieties come quickly to the fore.

Closely allied to 'Corner' on the one hand, and to 'Threadbare' on the other, is the marital game of 'Lunch Bag'. The husband, who can well afford to have lunch at a good restaurant, nevertheless makes himself a few sandwiches every morning, which he takes to the office in a paper bag. In this way he uses up crusts of bread, leftovers from dinner and paper bags which his wife saves for him. This gives him complete control over the family finances, for what wife would dare buy herself a mink stole in the face of such self-sacrifice? The husband reaps numerous other advantages, such as the privilege of eating lunch by himself and of catching up on his work during lunch hour. In many ways this is a constructive game which Benjamin Franklin would have approved of, since it encourages the virtues of thrift, hard work and punctuality.

2 · COURTROOM

Thesis. Descriptively this belongs to the class of games which find their most florid expressions in law, and which includes 'Wooden Leg' (the plea of insanity) and 'Debtor' (the civil suit). *Clinically* it is most often seen in marital counselling and marital psychotherapy groups. Indeed, some marital counselling and marital groups consist of a perpetual game of 'Courtroom' in which nothing is resolved, since the game is never broken up. In such cases it becomes evident that the counsellor or therapist is heavily involved in the game without being aware of it.

'Courtroom' can be played by any number, but is essentially three-handed, with a plaintiff, a defendant and a judge, represented by a husband, a wife and the therapist. If it is played in a therapy group or over the radio or TV, the other members of the audience are cast as the jury. The husband begins plaintively, 'Let me tell you what (wife's name) did yesterday. She took the . . .' etc., etc. The wife then responds defensively, 'Here is the way it really was . . . and besides just before that he was . . . and anyway at the time we were both . . .' etc. The husband adds gallantly, 'Well, I'm glad you people have a chance to hear both sides of the story, I only want to be fair.' At this point the counsellor says judiciously, 'It seems to me that if we consider . . .' etc., etc. If there is an audience, the therapist may throw it to them with: 'Well, let's hear what the others have to say.' Or, if the group is already trained, they will play the jury without any instruction from him.

Antithesis. The therapist says to the husband, 'You're absolutely right!' If the husband relaxes complacently or triumphantly, the therapist asks: 'How do you feel about my saying that?' The husband replies: 'Fine.' Then the therapist says, 'Actually, I feel you're in the wrong.' If the husband is honest, he will say: 'I knew that all along.' If he is not honest, he will show some reaction that makes it clear a game is in progress. Then it becomes possible to go into the matter further. The game element lies in the fact that while the plaintiff is overtly clamouring for victory, fundamentally he believes that he is wrong.

After sufficient clinical material has been gathered to clarify the situation, the game can be interdicted by a manoeuvre which is one of the most elegant in the whole art of antithetics. The therapist makes a rule prohibiting the use of the (grammatical) third person in the group. Thenceforward the members can only address each other directly as 'you' or talk about themselves as 'I', but they cannot say, 'Let me tell you about him' or 'Let me tell you about her'. At this point the couple stop playing games in the group altogether, or shift into 'Sweetheart' which is some improvement or take up 'Furthermore' which is no help at all. 'Sweetheart' is described in another section (page 94). In 'Furthermore' the plaintiff makes one accusation after the other. The defendant replies to each 'I can explain'. The plaintiff pays no attention to the explanation, but as soon as the defendant pauses, he launches into his next indictment with another 'furthermore', which is followed by another explanation – a typical Parent-Child interchange.

'Furthermore' is played most intensively by paranoid defendants. Because of their literalness, it is particularly easy for them to frustrate accusers who express themselves in humorous or metaphorical terms. In general, metaphors are the most obvious traps to avoid in a game of 'Furthermore'.

In its *everyday* form, 'Courtroom' is easily observed in children as a three-handed game between two siblings and a parent. 'Mummy, she took my candy away.' 'Yes, but he took my doll, and before that he was hitting me, and anyway we both promised to share our candy.'

ANALYSIS

Thesis: They've got to say I'm right.

Aim: Reassurance.

Roles: Plaintiff, Defendant, Judge (and/or Jury).

Dynamics: Sibling rivalry.

Examples: (1) Children quarrelling, parent intervenes. (2) Married couple, seek 'help'.

Social Paradigm: Adult-Adult.

　Adult: 'This is what she did to me.'

　Adult: 'The real facts are these.'

Psychological Paradigm: Child-Parent.

　Child: 'Tell *me* I'm right.'

　Parent: 'This one is right.' Or: 'You're both right.'

Moves: (1) Complaint filed – Defence filed. (2) Plaintiff files rebuttal, concession, or good-will gesture. (3) Decision of judge or instructions to jury. (4) Final decision filed.

Advantages: (1) Internal Psychological – projection of guilt. (2) External Psychological – excused from guilt. (3) Internal Social – 'Sweetheart', 'Furthermore', 'Uproar' and others. (4) External Social – 'Courtroom'. (5) Biological – stroking from judge and jury. (6) Existential – depressive position, I'm always wrong.

3 · FRIGID WOMAN

Thesis. This is almost always a marital game, since it is hardly conceivable that an informal liaison would present the required opportunities and privileges over a sufficient length of time, or that such a liaison would be maintained in the face of it.

The husband makes advances to his wife and is repulsed. After repeated attempts, he is told that all men are beasts, he doesn't really love her, or doesn't love her for herself, that all he is interested in is sex. He desists for a time, then tries again with the same result. Eventually he resigns himself and makes no further advances. As the weeks or months pass, the wife becomes increasingly informal and sometimes forgetful. She walks through the bedroom half dressed or forgets her clean towel when she takes a bath so that he has to bring it to her. If she plays a hard game or drinks heavily, she may become flirtatious with other men at parties. At length he responds to those provocations and tries again. Once more he is repulsed, and a game of 'Uproar' ensues involving their recent behaviour, other couples, their in-laws, their finances and their failures, terminated by a slamming door.

This time the husband makes up his mind that he is really through, that they will find a sexless *modus vivendi*. Months pass. He declines the negligee parade and the forgotten towel manoeuvre. The wife becomes more provocatively informal and more provocatively forgetful, but he still resists. Then one evening she actually approaches him and kisses him. At first he doesn't respond, remembering his resolution, but soon nature begins to take its course after the long famine, and now he thinks he surely has it made. His first tentative advances are not repulsed. He becomes bolder and bolder. Just at the critical point, the wife steps back and cries: 'See, what did I tell you! All men are beasts, all I wanted was affection, but all you are interested in is sex!' The ensuing game of 'Uproar' at this point may skip the preliminary phases of their recent behaviour and their in-laws, and go right to the financial problem.

It should be noted that in spite of his protestations, the husband is usually just as afraid of sexual intimacy as his wife is, and had carefully chosen his mate to minimize the danger of overtaxing his disturbed potency, which he can now blame on her.

In its *everyday* form this game is played by unmarried ladies of various ages, which soon earns them a common slang epithet. With them it often merges into the game of indignation, or 'Rapo'.

Antithesis. This is a dangerous game, and the possible antitheses are equally dangerous. Taking a mistress is a gamble. In the face of such stimulating competition, the wife may give up the game and try to initiate a normal married life, perhaps too late, On the other hand, she may use the affair, often with the help of a lawyer, as ammunition against the husband in a game of 'Now I've Got You, You Son of a Bitch'. The outcome is equally unpredictable if the husband undertakes psychotherapy and she does not. The wife's game may collapse as the husband grows stronger, leading to healthier adjustment; but if she is a hard player, improvement on his part may result in divorce. The best solution, if available, is for both parties to go into a transactional marital group, where the underlying advantages of the game and the basic sexual pathology can be laid bare. With this preparation both spouses may become interested in intensive individual psychotherapy. That may result in a psychological remarriage. If not, at least each of the parties may make a more sensible readjustment to the situation than they might have otherwise.

The decent antithesis for the *everyday* form is to find another social companion. Some of the shrewder or more brutal antitheses are corrupt and even criminal.

Relatives. The converse game, 'Frigid Man', is less common, but it takes much the same general course with some variations in detail. The final outcome depends upon the scripts of the parties involved.

The crucial point of 'Frigid Woman' is the terminal phase of 'Uproar'. Once this has run its course, sexual intimacy is out of the question, since both parties derive a perverse satisfaction from 'Uproar' and have no need of further sexual excitement from each other. Hence the most important item in anti-'Frigid Woman' is to decline 'Uproar'. This leaves the wife in a state of sexual dissatisfaction which may be so acute that she will become more compliant. The use made of 'Uproar' distinguishes 'Frigid Woman' from 'Beat Me Daddy', where 'Uproar' is part of the foreplay; in 'Frigid Woman', 'Uproar' substitutes for the sex act itself. Thus in 'Beat Me Daddy', 'Uproar' is a condition of the sexual act, a kind of fetish which increases the excitement, while in 'Frigid Woman', once 'Uproar' has taken place, the episode is finished.

An early analogue of 'Frigid Woman' is played by that type of prissy little girl described by Dickens in *Great Expectations*. She comes out in her starched dress and asks the little boy to make her a mud pie. Then she sneers at his dirty hands and clothing and tells him how clean she is.

ANALYSIS

Thesis: Now I've got you, you son of a bitch.
Aim: Vindication.
Roles: Proper Wife, Inconsiderate Husband.
Dynamics: Penis envy.
Examples: (1) Thank you for the mud pie, you dirty little boy.
(2) Provocative, frigid wife.
Social Paradigm: Parent-Child.

Parent: 'I give you permission to make me a mud pie (kiss me).'

Child: 'I'd love to.'

Parent: 'Now see how dirty you are.'

Psychological Paradigm: Child-Parent.

Child: 'See if you can seduce me.'

Parent: 'I'll try, if you stop me.'

Child: 'See, it was you who started it.'

Moves: (1) Seduction-Response. (2) Rejection-Resignation. (3) Provocation-Response. (4) Rejection-Uproar.

Advantages: (1) Internal Psychological – freedom from guilt for sadistic fantasies. (2) External Psychological – avoids feared exhibition and penetration. (3) Internal Social – 'Uproar'. (4) External Social – What do you do with dirty little boys (husbands)? (5) Biological – inhibited sex play and belligerent exchanges. (6) Existential – I am pure.

4 · HARRIED

Thesis. This is a game played by the harried housewife. Her situation requires that she be proficient in ten or twelve different occupations; or, stated otherwise, that she fill gracefully ten or twelve different roles. From time to time semi-facetious lists of these occupations or roles appear in the Sunday supplements: mistress, mother, nurse, housemaid, etc. Since these roles are usually conflicting and fatiguing, their imposition gives rise in the course of years to the condition symbolically known as 'Housewife's Knee' (since the knee is used for rocking, scrubbing, lifting, driving and so forth), whose symptoms are succinctly summarized in the complaint: 'I'm tired.'

Now, if the housewife is able to set her own pace and find enough satisfaction in loving her husband and children, she will not merely serve but enjoy her twenty-five years, and see the youngest child off to college with a pang of loneliness. But if on the one hand she is driven by her inner Parent and called to account by the critical husband she has chosen for that purpose, and on the other unable to get sufficient satisfaction from loving her family, she may grow more and more unhappy. At first she may try to console herself with the advantages of 'If It Weren't For You' and 'Blemish' (and indeed, any housewife may fall back on these when the going gets rough); but soon these fail to keep her going. Then she has to find another way out, and that is the game of 'Harried'.

The thesis of this game is simple. She takes on everything that comes, and even asks for more. She agrees with her husband's criticisms and accepts all her children's demands. If she has to entertain at dinner, she not only feels she must function impeccably as a conversationalist, chatelaine over the household and servants, interior decorator, caterer, glamour girl, virgin queen and diplomat; she will also volunteer that morning to bake a cake and take the children to the dentist. If she already feels harassed, she makes the day even more harried. Then in the middle of the afternoon she justifiably collapses, and nothing gets done. She lets down her husband, the children and their guests, and her self-reproaches add to her misery. After this happens two or three times her marriage is in jeopardy, the children are confused, she loses weight, her hair is untidy, her face is drawn and her shoes are scuffed. Then she appears at the psychiatrist's office, ready to be hospitalized.

Antithesis. The logical antithesis is simple: Mrs White can fill each of her roles in succession during the week, but she must refuse to play two or more of them simultaneously. When she gives a cocktail party, for example, she can play either caterer or nursemaid, but not both. If she is merely suffering from Housewife's Knee, she may be able to limit herself in this way.

If she is actually playing a game of 'Harried', however, it will be very difficult for her to adhere to this principle. In that case the husband is carefully chosen; he is an otherwise reasonable man who will criticize his wife if she is not as efficient as he thinks his mother was. In effect, she marries his fantasy of his mother as perpetuated in his Parent, which is similar to her fantasy of her mother or grandmother. Having found a suitable partner, her Child can now settle into the harassed role necessary to maintain her psychic balance, and which she will not readily give up. The more occupational responsibility the husband has, the easier it is for both of them to find Adult reasons to preserve the unhealthy aspects of their relationship.

When the position becomes untenable, often because of official school intervention on behalf of the unhappy offspring, the psychiatrist is called in to make it a three-handed game. Either the husband wants him to do an overhaul job on the wife, or the wife wants him as an ally against the husband. The ensuing proceedings depend on the skill and alertness of the psychiatrist. Usually the first phase, the alleviation of the wife's depression, will proceed smoothly. The second phase, in which she will give up playing 'Harried' in favour of playing 'Psychiatry', is the decisive one. It tends to arouse increasing opposition from both spouses. Sometimes this is well concealed and then explodes suddenly, though not unexpectedly. If this stage is weathered, then the real work of game analysis can proceed.

It is necessary to recognize that the real culprit is the wife's Parent, her mother or grandmother; the husband is to some extent only a lay figure chosen to play his role in the game. The therapist has to fight not only this Parent and the husband, who has a heavy investment in playing his end, but also the social environment, which encourages the wife's compliance. The week after the article appears about the many roles a housewife has to play, there is a *How'm I Doing?* in the Sunday paper: a ten-item test to determine 'How Good A Hostess (Wife) (Mother) (Housekeeper) (Budgeteer) Are You?' For the housewife who plays 'Harried', that is the equivalent of the little leaflet that comes with children's games, stating the rules. It may help to speed up the evolution of 'Harried', which, if not checked, may end in a game of 'State Hospital' ('The last thing I want is to be sent to a hospital').

One practical difficulty with such couples is that the husband tends to avoid personal involvement with the treatment beyond playing 'Look How Hard I'm Trying', because he is usually more disturbed than he cares to admit. Instead he may send indirect messages to the therapist, through temper outbursts which he knows will be reported by the wife. Hence 'Harried' easily progresses to a third-degree life-death-divorce struggle. The psychiatrist is almost alone on the side of life, assisted only by the harried Adult of the patient which is locked in combat that may prove mortal against all three aspects of the husband, allied with her own inner Parent and Child. It is a dramatic battle, with odds of two against five, which tries the skill of the most game-free and professional therapist. If he quails, he can take the easy way out and offer his patient on the altar of the divorce court, which is equivalent to saying 'I surrender – Let's you and him fight.'

5 · IF IT WEREN'T FOR YOU

Thesis. The detailed analysis of this game has already been given in Chapter 5. It was historically the second game uncovered, after 'Why Don't You – Yes But', which up to that point had been regarded merely as an interesting phenomenon. With the additional discovery of IWFY, it became clear that there must be a whole department of social action based on ulterior transactions. This led to a more active search for such goings-on, and the present collection is one outcome.

Briefly, a woman marries a domineering man so that he will restrict her activities and thus keep her from getting into situations which frighten her. If this were a simple operation, she might express her gratitude when he performed this service for her. In the game of IWFY, however, her reaction is quite the opposite: she takes advantage of the situation to complain about the restrictions, which makes her spouse feel uneasy and gives her all sorts of advantages. This game is the internal social advantage. The external social advantage is the derivative pastime 'If It Weren't For Him', which she plays with her congenial lady friends.

6 · LOOK HOW HARD I'VE TRIED

Thesis. In its common *clinical* form this is a three-handed game played by a married couple with a psychiatrist. The husband (usually) is bucking for a divorce, despite loud protestations to the contrary, while the spouse is more sincere in wanting to continue the marriage. He comes to the therapist under protest and talks just enough to demonstrate to the wife that he is cooperating; usually he plays a mild game of 'Psychiatry' or 'Courtroom'. As time passes he exhibits either increasingly resentful pseudo-compliance or belligerent argumentativeness towards the therapist. At home he initially shows more 'understanding' and restraint, and finally behaves worse than ever. After one, five or ten visits, depending on the skill of the therapist, he refuses to come any longer and goes hunting or fishing instead. The wife is then forced into filing for divorce. The husband is now blameless, since his wife has taken the initiative and he has demonstrated his good faith by going to the therapist. He is in a good position to say to any attorney, judge, friend or relative, 'Look how hard I've tried!'

Antithesis. The couple is seen together. If one – let us say the husband – is clearly playing this game, the other is taken into individual treatment and the player is sent on his way, on the valid ground that he is less ready for therapy. He can still get a divorce, but only at the expense of abandoning his position that he is really trying. If necessary, the wife can start the divorce, and her position is much improved since she really has tried. The favourable, hoped-for outcome is that the husband, his game broken up, will go into a state of despair and then seek treatment elsewhere with genuine motivation.

In its *everyday* form this is easily observed in children as a two-handed game with one parent. It is played from either of two positions: 'I am helpless' or 'I am blameless'. The child tries, but bungles or is unsuccessful. If he is Helpless, the parent has to do it for him. If he is Blameless, the parent has no reasonable grounds for punishing him. This reveals the elements of the game. The parents should find out two things: which of them taught the child this game; and what they are doing to perpetuate it.

An interesting, though sometimes sinister, variant is 'Look How Hard I Was Trying', which is usually a harder game of the second or third degree. This can be illustrated by the case of a hard-working man with a gastric ulcer. There are many people with progressive physical disabilities who do the best they can to cope with the situation, and they may enlist the help of their families in a legitimate way. Such conditions, however, can also be exploited for ulterior purposes.

First Degree: A man announces to his wife and friends that he has an ulcer. He also lets them know that he is continuing to work. This elicits their admiration. Perhaps a person with a painful and unpleasant condition is entitled to a certain amount of ostentation as a poor recompense for his suffering. He should be given due credit for not playing 'Wooden Leg' instead, and deserves some reward for continuing to assume his responsibilities. In such a case, the courteous reply to 'Look How Hard I'm Trying' is, 'Yes, we all admire your fortitude and conscientiousness.'

Second Degree: A man is told that he has an ulcer, but keeps it a secret from his wife and friends. He continues working and worrying as hard as ever, and one day he collapses on the job. When his wife is notified, she gets the message instantly: 'Look

How Hard I Was Trying.' Now she is supposed to appreciate him as she never has before, and to feel sorry for all the mean things she has said and done in the past. In short, she is now supposed to love him, all previous methods of wooing her having failed. Unfortunately for the husband, her manifestations of affection and solicitude at this point are more apt to be motivated by guilt than by love. Deep down she is likely to be resentful because he is using unfair leverage against her, and has also taken unfair advantage of her by keeping his illness a secret. In short, a diamond bracelet is a much more honest instrument of courtship than a perforated stomach. She has the option of throwing the jewellery back at him, but she cannot decently walk out on the ulcer. A sudden confrontation with a serious illness is more likely to make her feel trapped than won over.

This game can often be discovered immediately after the patient first hears that he has a potentially progressive disability. If he is going to play it, the whole plan will very likely flash through his mind at that point, and can be recovered by a careful psychiatric review of the situation. What is recovered is the secret gloating of his Child at learning that he has such a weapon, masked by his Adult concern at the practical problems raised by his illness.

Third Degree: Even more sinister and spiteful is the sudden unheralded suicide because of serious illness. The ulcer progresses to cancer, and one day the wife, who has never been informed that anything serious is amiss, walks into the bathroom and finds her husband lying there dead. The note says clearly enough, 'Look How Hard I Was Trying.' If something like this happens twice to the same woman, it is time for her to find out what she has been playing.

ANALYSIS

Thesis: They can't push me around.
Aim: Vindication.
Roles: Standfast, Persecutor, Authority.
Dynamics: Anal passivity.
Examples: (1) Child dressing. (2) Spouse bucking for divorce.
Social Paradigm: Adult-Adult.

Adult: 'It's time to (get dressed) (go to a psychiatrist).'
Adult: 'All right, I'll try it.'

Psychological Paradigm: Parent-Child.

Parent: 'I'm going to make you (get dressed) (go to a psychiatrist).'

Child: 'See, it doesn't work.'

Moves: (1) Suggestion-Resistance. (2) Pressure-Compliance. (3) Approval-Failure.

Advantages: (1) Internal Psychological – freedom from guilt for aggression. (2) External Psychological – evades domestic responsibilities. (3) Internal Social – Look how hard I've tried. (4) External Social – same. (5) Biological – belligerent exchanges. (6) Existential – I am helpless (blameless).

7 · SWEETHEART

Thesis. This is seen in its fullest flower in the early stages of marital group therapy, when the parties feel defensive; it can also be observed on social occasions. White makes a subtly derogatory remark about Mrs White, disguised as an anecdote, and ends: 'Isn't that right, sweetheart?' Mrs White tends to agree for two ostensibly Adult reasons: (*a*) because the anecdote itself is in the main, accurately reported, and to disagree about what is presented as a peripheral detail (but is really the essential point of the transaction) would seem pedantic; (*b*) because it would seem surly to disagree with a man who calls one 'sweetheart' in public. The psychological reason for her agreement, however, is her depressive position. She married him precisely because she knew he would perform this service for her: exposing her deficiencies and thus saving her from the embarrassment of having to expose them herself. Her parents accommodated her the same way when she was little.

Next to 'Courtroom', this is the most common game played in marital groups. The more tense the situation, and the closer the game is to exposure, the more bitterly is the word 'sweetheart' enunciated, until the underlying resentment becomes obvious. On careful consideration it can be seen that this is a relative of 'Schlemiel', since the significant move is Mrs White's implicit forgiveness for White's resentment, of which she is trying hard not to be aware. Hence anti-'Sweetheart' is played analogously to anti-'Schlemiel': 'You can tell derogatory anecdotes about me, but please don't call me "sweetheart".' This antithesis carries with it the same perils as does anti-'Schlemiel'. A more sophisticated and less dangerous antithesis is to reply: 'Yes, *honey*!'

In another form the wife, instead of agreeing, responds with a similar 'Sweetheart' type anecdote about the husband, saying in effect, 'You have a dirty face too, dear.'

Sometimes the endearments are not actually pronounced, but a careful listener can hear them even when they are unspoken. This is 'Sweetheart', Silent Type.

REFERENCE

1. Bateson, G., *et al.*, 'Toward a Theory of Schizophrenia', *Behavioral Science*, 1: 251–264, 1956.

8 · Party Games

PARTIES are for pastimes, and pastimes are for parties (including the period before a group meeting officially begins), but as acquaintanceship ripens, games begin to emerge. The Schlemiel and his victim recognize each other, as do Big Daddy and Little Old Me; all the familiar but disregarded processes of selection get under way. In this section four games which are typically played in ordinary social situations are considered: 'Ain't It Awful', 'Blemish', 'Schlemiel', and 'Why Don't You – Yes But'.

1 · AIN'T IT AWFUL

Thesis. This is played in four significant forms: Parental pastime, Adult pastime, Child pastime and game. In the pastimes there is no denouement or payoff, but much unworthy feeling.

1. 'Nowadays' is the self-righteous, punitive or even vicious Parental pastime. Sociologically it is common among certain types of middle-aged women with small independent incomes. One such woman withdrew from a therapy group when her opening move was met with silence instead of with the excited corroboration she was accustomed to in her social circle. In this more sophisticated group, accustomed to game analysis, there was a conspicuous lack of togetherness when White remarked: 'Speaking of not trusting people, it's no wonder you can't trust anyone nowadays. I was looking through the desk of one of my roomers, and you won't believe what I found.' She knew the answers to most of the current community problems: juvenile delinquency (parents too soft nowadays); divorce (wives without enough to do to keep them busy nowadays); crime (foreigners moving into white neighbourhoods nowadays); and rising prices (businessmen too grasping nowadays). She made it clear that she herself was not soft with her delinquent son, nor with her delinquent tenants.

'Nowadays' is differentiated from idle gossip by its slogan 'It's no wonder'. The opening move may be the same ('They say that Flossie Murgatroyd'), but in 'Nowadays' there is direction and closure; an 'explanation' may be offered. Idle gossip merely rambles or trails off.

2. 'Broken Skin' is the more benevolent Adult variation, with the slogan 'What a pity!' although the underlying motivations are equally morbid. 'Broken Skin' deals primarily with the flow of blood; it is essentially an informal clinical colloquium. Anyone is eligible to present a case, the more horrifying the better, and details are eagerly considered. Blows in the face, abdominal operations and difficult childbirths are accepted topics. Here the differentiation from idle gossip lies in the rivalry and surgical sophistication. Pathological anatomy, diagnosis, prognosis and comparative case studies are systematically pursued. A good prognosis is approved in idle gossip, but in 'Broken Skin' a consistently hopeful outlook, unless obviously insincere, may invoke a secret meeting of the Credentials Committee because the player is *non particeps criminis*.

3. 'Water Cooler', or 'Coffee Break', is the Child pastime, with the slogan 'Look what they're doing to us now.' This is an organizational variant. It may be played after dark in the milder political or economic form called 'Bar Stool'. It is actually three-handed, the ace being held by the often shadowy figure called 'They'.

4. As a game, 'Ain't It Awful' finds its most dramatic expression in polysurgery addicts, and their transactions illustrate its characteristics. These are doctor-shoppers, people who actively seek surgery even in the face of sound medical opposition. The experience itself, the hospitalization and surgery, brings its own advantages. The internal psychological advantage comes from having the body mutilated; the external psychological advantage lies in the avoidance of all intimacies and responsibilities except complete surrender to the surgeon. The biological advantages are typified by nursing care. The internal social advantages come from the medical and nursing staff, and from other patients. After the patient's discharge the external social advantages are gained by provoking sympathy and awe. In its extreme form this game is played professionally by fraudulent or determined liability and malpractice claimants, who may earn a living by deliberately or opportunistically incurring disabilities. They then demand not only sympathy, as amateur players do, but indemnification. 'Ain't It Awful' becomes a game, then, when the player overtly expresses

distress, but is covertly gratified at the prospect of the satisfactions he can wring from his misfortune.

In general, people who suffer misfortunes may be divided into three classes.

1. Those in whom the suffering is inadvertent and unwanted. These may or may not exploit the sympathy which is so readily offered to them. Some exploitation is natural enough, and may be treated with common courtesy.

2. Those in whom the suffering is inadvertent, but is gratefully received because of the opportunities for exploitation it offers. Here the game is an afterthought, a 'secondary grain' in Freud's sense.

3. Those who seek suffering, like polysurgery addicts who go from one surgeon to another until they find one willing to operate. Here the game is the primary consideration.

2 · BLEMISH

Thesis. This game is the source of a large percentage of petty dissension in everyday life; it is played from the depressive Child position 'I am no good', which is protectively transformed into the Parental position 'They are no good.' The player's transactional problem is, then, to prove the latter thesis. Hence 'Blemish' players do not feel comfortable with a new person until they have found his blemish. In its hardest form it may become a totalitarian political game played by 'authoritarian' personalities, and then it may have serious historical repercussions. Here its close relationship with 'Nowadays' is evident. In suburban society positive reassurance is obtained from playing 'How'm I Doing?' while 'Blemish' provides negative reassurance. A partial analysis will make some of the elements of this game clearer.

The premise may range from the most trivial and extraneous ('Last year's hat'), to the most cynical ('Hasn't got $7,000 in the bank'), sinister ('Not 100% Aryan'), esoteric ('Hasn't read Rilke') intimate ('Can't hold his erection') or sophisticated ('What's he trying to prove?'). Psychodynamically it is usually based on sexual insecurity, and its aim is reassurance. Transactionally there is prying, morbid curiosity or watchfulness, sometimes with Parental or Adult concern charitably masking the Child's relish. It has the internal psychological advantage of warding off depression, and the external psychological advantage of avoiding the intimacy which might expose White's own blemishes. White feels justified in turning away an unfashionable woman, a man without financial backing, a non-Aryan, an illiterate, an impotent man or an insecure personality. At the same time the prying offers some internal social action with biological gain. The external social advantage is of the 'Ain't It Awful' family – Neighbourly Type.

An interesting sidelight is that White's choice of premise is independent of his intellectual capacity or apparent sophistication. Thus a man who had held some responsible positions in the foreign service of his country told an audience that another country was inferior because, among other things, the men wore jackets with sleeves that were too long. In his Adult ego state this man was quite competent. Only when playing a Parental game like 'Blemish' would he mention such irrelevancies.

3 · SCHLEMIEL

Thesis. The term 'schlemiel' does not refer to the hero of Chamisso's novel,[1] who was a man without a shadow, but to a popular Yiddish word allied to the German and Dutch words for cunning. The Schlemiel's victim, who is something like the 'Good-Natured Fellow' of Paul de Kock,[2] is colloquially called the Schlemazl. The moves in a typical game of 'Schlemiel' are as follows:

1W. White spills a highball on the hostess's evening gown.

1B. Black (the host) responds initially with rage, but he senses (often only vaguely) that if he shows it, White wins. Black therefore pulls himself together, and this gives him the illusion that he wins.

2W. White says: 'I'm sorry.'

2B. Black mutters or cries forgiveness, strengthening his illusion that he wins.

3W. White then proceeds to inflict other damage on Black's property. He breaks things, spills things and makes messes of various kinds. After the cigarette burn in the tablecloth, the chair leg through the lace curtain and the gravy on the rug, White's Child is exhilarated because he has enjoyed himself in carrying out these procedures, for all of which he has been forgiven, while Black has made a gratifying display of suffering self-control. Thus both of them profit from an unfortunate situation, and Black is not necessarily anxious to terminate the friendship.

As in most games, White, who makes the first move, wins either way. If Black shows his anger, White can feel justified in returning the resentment. If Black restrains himself, White can go on enjoying his opportunities. The real payoff in this game, however, is not the pleasure of destructiveness, which is merely an added bonus for White, but the fact that he obtains forgiveness.* This leads directly into the antithesis.

Antithesis. Anti-'Schlemiel' is played by not offering the demanded absolution. After White says 'I'm sorry', Black, instead of muttering 'It's okay', says, 'Tonight you can embarrass my wife, ruin the furniture and wreck the rug, but please don't say "I'm sorry".' Here Black switches from being a forgiving Parent to being an objective Adult who takes the full responsibility for having invited White in the first place.

The intensity of White's game will be revealed by his reaction, which may be quite explosive. One who plays anti-'Schlemiel' runs the risk of immediate reprisals or, at any rate, of making an enemy.

Children play 'Schlemiel' in an abortive form in which they are not always sure of forgiveness but at least have the pleasure of making messes; as they learn to comport themselves socially, however, they may take advantage of their increasing sophistication to obtain the forgiveness which is the chief goal of the game as played in polite, grown-up social circles.

ANALYSIS

Thesis: I can be destructive and still get forgiveness.

Aim: Absolution.

Roles: Aggressor, Victim (colloquially, Schlemiel and Schlemazl).

Dynamics: Anal aggression.

Examples: (1) Messily destructive children. (2) Clumsy guest.

Social Paradigm: Adult-Adult.

   Adult: 'Since I'm polite, you have to be polite, too.'
   Adult: 'That's fine. I forgive you.'

* The examples given for this and the next game (YDYB) follow those given previously by the author in *Transactional Analysis*.

Psychological Paradigm: Child-Parent.

Child: 'You have to forgive things which appear accidental.'

Parent: 'You are right. I have to show you what good manners are.'

Moves: (1) Provocation-resentment. (2) Apology-forgiveness.

Advantages: (1) Internal Psychological – pleasure of messing. (2) External Psychological – Avoids punishment. (3) Internal Social – 'Schlemiel.' (4) External Social – 'Schlemiel.' (5) Biological – provocative and gentle stroking. (6) Existential – I am blameless.

4 · WHY DON'T YOU '- YES BUT

Thesis. 'Why Don't You – Yes But' occupies a special place in game analysis, because it was the original stimulus for the concept of games. It was the first game to be dissected out of its social context, and since it is the oldest subject of game analysis, it is one of the best understood. It is also the game most commonly played at parties and in groups of all kinds, including psychotherapy groups. The following example will serve to illustrate its main characteristics:

White: 'My husband always insists on doing our own repairs, and he never builds anything right.'

Black: 'Why doesn't he take a course in carpentry?'

White: 'Yes, but he doesn't have time.'

Blue: 'Why don't you buy him some good tools?'

White: 'Yes, but he doesn't know how to use them.'

Red: 'Why don't you have your building done by a carpenter?'

White: 'Yes, but that would cost too much.'

Brown: 'Why don't you just accept what he does the way he does it?'

White: 'Yes, but the whole thing might fall down.'

Such an exchange is typically followed by a silence. It is eventually broken by Green, who may say something like, 'That's men for you, aways trying to show how efficient they are.'

YDYB can be played by any number. The agent presents a problem. The others start to present solutions, each beginning with 'Why don't you . . . ?' To each of these White objects with a 'Yes, but . . .' A good player can stand off the others indefinitely until they all give up, whereupon White wins. In many situations she might have to handle a dozen or more solutions to engineer the crestfallen silence which signifies her victory, and which leaves the field open for the next game in the above paradigm, Green switching into 'PTA', Delinquent Husband Type.

Since the solutions are, with rare exceptions, rejected, it is apparent that this game must serve some ulterior purpose. YDYB is not played for its ostensible purpose (an Adult quest for information or solutions), but to reassure and gratify the Child. A bare

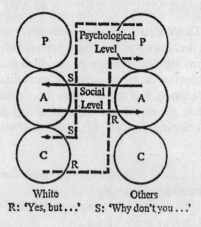

White   Others
R: 'Yes, but...'   S: 'Why don't you ...'

Figure 8. Why Don't You – Yes But

transcript may sound Adult, but in the living tissue it can be observed that White presents herself as a Child inadequate to meet the situation; whereupon the others become transformed into sage Parents anxious to dispense their wisdom for her benefit.

This is illustrated in Figure 8. The game can proceed because at the social level both stimulus and response are Adult to Adult, and at the psychological level they are also complementary, with Parent to Child stimulus ('Why don't you . . .') eliciting Child to Parent response ('Yes, but . . .'). The psychological level is usually unconscious on both sides, but the shifts in ego state (Adult to 'inadequate' Child on White's part, Adult to 'wise' Parent by the others) can often be detected by an alert observer from changes in posture, muscular tone, voice and vocabulary.

In order to illustrate the implications, it is instructive to follow through on the example given above.

Therapist: 'Did anyone suggest anything you hadn't thought of yourself?'

White: 'No, they didn't. As a matter of fact, I've actually tried almost everything they suggested. I did buy my husband some tools, and he did take a course in carpentry.'

Here White demonstrates two of the reasons why the proceedings should not be taken at face value. First, in the majority of cases White is as intelligent as anyone else in the company, and it is very unlikely that others will suggest any solution that she has not thought of herself. If someone does happen to come up with an original suggestion, White will accept it gratefully if she is playing fair; that is, her 'inadequate' Child will give way if anyone present has an idea ingenious enough to stimulate her Adult. But habitual YDYB players, such as White above, seldom play fair. On the other hand, a too ready acceptance of suggestions raises the question of whether the YDYB is not masking an underlying game of 'Stupid'.

The example given is particularly dramatic, because it clearly illustrates the second point. Even if White has actually tried some of the solutions presented, she will still object to them. The purpose of the game is not to get suggestions, but to reject them.

While almost anyone will play this game under proper circumstances because of its time-structuring value, careful study of individuals who particularly favour it reveals several interesting features. First, they characteristically can and will play either side of the game with equal facility. This switchability of roles is true of all games. Players may habitually prefer one role to another, but they are capable of trading, and they are willing to play any other role in the same game if for some reason that is indicated. (Compare, for example, the switch from Drinker to Rescuer in the game of 'Alcoholic'.)

Second, in clinical practice it is found that people who favour YDYB belong to that class of patients who eventually request hypnosis or some sort of hypnotic injection as a method of speeding up their treatment. When they are playing the game, their object is to demonstrate that no one can give them an acceptable suggestion – that is, they will never surrender; whereas with the therapist, they request a procedure which will put them in a state of complete surrender. It is thus apparent that YDYB represents a social solution to a conflict about surrender.

Even more specifically, this game is common among people who have a fear of blushing, as the following therapeutic exchange demonstrates:

Therapist: 'Why do you play "Why Don't You – Yes But" if you know it's a con?'

White: 'If I'm talking to somebody I have to keep thinking of things to say. If I don't, I'll blush. Except in the dark. I can't stand a lull. I know it, and my husband knows it, too. He's always told me that.'

Therapist: 'You mean if your Adult doesn't keep busy, your Child takes the chance to pop up and make you feel embarrassed?'

White: 'That's it. So if I can keep making suggestions to somebody, or get him to make suggestions to me, then I'm all right, I'm protected. As long as I can keep my Adult in control, I can postpone the embarrassment.'

Here White indicates clearly that she fears unstructured time. Her Child is prevented from advertising as long as the Adult can be kept busy in a social situation, and a game offers a suitable structure for Adult functioning. But the game must be suitably motivated in order to maintain her interest. Her choice of YDYB is influenced by the principle of economy: it yields the maximum internal and external advantages to her Child's conflicts about physical passivity. She could play with equal zest either the shrewd Child who cannot be dominated or the sage Parent who tries to dominate the Child in someone else, but fails. Since the basic principle of YDYB is that no suggestion is ever accepted, the Parent is never successful. The motto of the game is: 'Don't get panicky, the Parent never succeeds.'

In summary, then: while each move is amusing, so to speak, to White, and brings its own little pleasure in rejecting the suggestion, the real payoff is the silence or masked silence which ensues when all the others have racked their brains and grown tired of trying to think of acceptable solutions. This signifies to White and to them that she has won by demonstrating it is they who are inadequate. If the silence is not masked, it may persist for several minutes. In the paradigm, Green cut White's triumph short because of her eagerness to start a game of her own, and that was what kept her from participating in White's game. Later on in the session, White demonstrated her resentment against Green for having abridged her moment of victory.

Another curious feature of YDYB is that the external and internal games are played exactly the same way, with the roles reversed. In the external form, the one observed clinically, White's Child comes out to play the role of the inadequate help-seeker in a many-handed situation. In the internal form, the more intimate two-handed game played at home with her husband, her Parent comes out as the wise, efficient suggestion-giver. This reversal is usually secondary, however, since during the courtship she plays the helpless Child side, and only after the honeymoon is over does her bossy Parent begin to emerge into the open. There may have been slips as the wedding approached, but her fiancé will overlook these in his eagerness to settle down with his carefully chosen bride. If he does not overlook them, the engagement may be called off for 'good reasons', and White, sadder but no wiser, will resume her search for a suitable mate.

Antithesis. It is evident that those who respond to White's first move, the presentation of her 'problem', are playing a form of 'I'm Only Trying to Help You' (ITHY). In fact YDYB is the inverse of ITHY. In ITHY there is one therapist and many clients; in YDYB one client and many 'therapists'. The clinical antithesis to YDYB, therefore, is not to play ITHY. If the opening is of the form: 'What do you do if . . .' (WYDI), a suggested response is: 'That *is* a difficult problem. What *are* you going to do about it?' If it is of the form: 'X didn't work out properly', the response then should be 'That *is* too bad.' Both of these are polite enough to leave White at a loss, or at least to elicit a crossed transaction, so that his frustration becomes manifest and can then be explored. In a therapy group it is good practice for susceptible patients to refrain from playing ITHY when invited. Then not only White, but the other members as well, can learn from anti-YDYB, which is merely the other side of anti-ITHY.

In a social situation, if the game is friendly and harmless, there is no reason not to participate. If it is an attempt to exploit professional knowledge, an antithetical move may be required; but in such situations this arouses resentment because of the exposure of White's Child. The best policy under those circumstances is to flee from the opening move and look for a stimulating game of first-degree 'Rapo'.

Relatives. 'Why Don't You – Yes But' must be distinguished from its obverse, 'Why Did You – No But' (YDNB), in which it is the Parent who wins and the defensive Child who eventually retires in confusion, although again the bare transcript may sound factual, rational and Adult to Adult. YDNB is closely related to 'Furthermore'.

The reverse of YDYB at first resembles 'Peasant'. Here White seduces the therapist into giving her suggestions which she immediately accepts, rather than rejects. Only after he is deeply involved does he perceive that White is turning on him. What looked like 'Peasant' ends up as a game of intellectual 'Rapo'. The classical version of this is the switch from positive to negative transference in the course of orthodox psychoanalysis.

YDYB may also be played in a second-degree hard form as 'Do Me Something'. The patient refuses to do the housework, for example, and there is a game of YDYB every evening, when the husband returns home. But no matter what he says, she sullenly refuses to change her ways. In some cases the sullenness may be malignant and require careful psychiatric evaluation. The game aspect must be considered as well, however, since it raises the question of why the husband selected such a spouse, and how he contributes to maintaining the situation.

ANALYSIS

Thesis: See if you can present a solution I can't find fault with.
Aim: Reassurance.
Roles: Helpless person, Advisers.
Dynamics: Surrender conflict (oral).
Examples: (1) Yes, but I can't do my homework now because ... (2) Helpless wife.
Social Paradigm: Adult-Adult.
 Adult: 'What do you do if . . .'
 Adult: 'Why don't you . . .'

Adult: 'Yes, but . . .'

Psychological Paradigm: Parent-Child.

Parent: 'I can make you grateful for my help.'

Child: 'Go ahead and try.'

Moves: (1) Problem-Solution. (2) Objection-Solution. (3) Objection-Disconcertion.

Advantages: (1) Internal Psychological – reassurance. (2) External Psychological – avoids surrender. (3) Internal Social – YDYB, Parental role. (4) External Social – YDYB, Child role. (5) Biological – rational discussion. (6) Existential – Everybody wants to dominate me.

REFERENCES

1. von Chamisso, Adelbert, *Peter Schlemiel*, Calder, 1957.

2. de Kock, Paul. One of the most popular works of this nineteenth-century librettist and novelist is *A Good-Natured Fellow*, about a man who gives away too much.

9 · Sexual Games

SOME games are played to exploit or fight off sexual impulses These are all, in effect, perversions of the sexual instincts in which the satisfaction is displaced from the sexual act to the crucial transactions which constitute the payoff of the game. This cannot always be demonstrated convincingly, because such games are usually played in privacy, so that clinical information about them has to be obtained secondhand, and the informant's bias cannot always be satisfactorily evaluated. The psychiatric conception of homosexuality, for example, is heavily skewed, because the more aggressive and successful 'players' do not often come for psychiatric treatment, and the available material mostly concerns the passive partners.

The games included here are: 'Let's You and Him Fight', 'Perversion', 'Rapo', 'Stocking Game' and 'Uproar'. In most cases the agent is a woman. This is because the hard forms of sexual games in which the man is the agent verge on or constitute criminality, and properly belong in the Underworld section. On the other side, sexual games and marital games overlap, but the ones described here are readily available to unmarried people as well as to spouses.

1 · LET'S YOU AND HIM FIGHT

Thesis. This may be a manoeuvre, a ritual or a game. In each case the psychology is essentially feminine. Because of its dramatic qualities, LYAHF is the basis of much of the world's literature, both good and bad.

1. As a manoeuvre it is romantic. The woman manoeuvres or challenges two men into fighting, with the implication or promise that she will surrender herself to the winner. After the competition is decided, she fulfils her bargain. This is an honest transaction, and the presumption is that she and her mate live happily ever after.

2. As a ritual, it tends to be tragic. Custom demands that the two men fight for her, even if she does not want them to, and even

if she has already made her choice. If the wrong man wins, she must nevertheless take him. In this case it is society and not the woman who sets up L Y A H F. If she is unwilling, the transaction is an honest one. If she is unwilling or disappointed, the outcome may offer her considerable scope for playing games, such as 'Let's Pull A Fast One on Joey'.

3. As a game it is comic. The woman sets up the competition, and while the two men are fighting, she decamps with a third. The internal and external psychological advantages for her and her mate are derived from the position that honest competition is for suckers, and the comic story they have lived through forms the basis for the internal and external social advantages.

2 · PERVERSION

Thesis. Heterosexual perversions such as fetishism, sadism and masochism are symptomatic of a confused Child and are treated accordingly. Their transactional aspects, however, as manifested in actual sexual situations, can be dealt with by means of game analysis. This may lead to social control, so that even if the warped sexual impulses remain unchanged, they are neutralized as far as actual indulgence is concerned.

People who are suffering from mild sadistic or masochistic distortions tend to take a primitive kind of 'Mental Health' position. They feel that they are strongly sexed, and that prolonged abstinence will lead to serious consequences. Neither of these conclusions is necessarily true, but they form the basis for a game of 'Wooden Leg' with the plea: 'What do you expect from someone as strongly sexed as I am?'

Antithesis. To extend ordinary courtesy to oneself and one's partner; that is, to refrain from verbal or physical flagellation and confine oneself to more conventional forms of coitus. If White is a true pervert, this will lay bare the second element of the game, which is often clearly expressed in his dreams: that coitus itself has little interest for him, and that his real satisfaction is derived from the humiliating foreplay. This is something that he may not have cared to admit to himself. But it will now become clear to him that his complaint is: 'After all this work, I have to have intercourse, yet!' At this point the position is much more favourable for specific psychotherapy, and much of the pleading and evasiveness has been nullified. This applies to ordinary 'sexual psychopaths' as seen in practice, and not to malignant schizophrenic or criminal perversions, nor to those who confine their sexual activities to fantasy.

The game of 'Homosexuality' has become elaborated into a subculture in many countries, just as it is ritualized in others. Many of the disabilities which result from homosexuality arise from making it into a game. The provocative behaviour which gives rise to 'Cops and Robbers', 'Why Does This Always Happen to Us', 'It's the Society We Live In', 'All Great Men Were' and so forth, is often amenable to social control, which reduces the handicaps to a minimum. The 'professional homosexual' wastes a large amount of time and energy which could be applied to other ends. Analysis of his games may help him establish a quiet ménage which will leave him free to enjoy the benefits that bourgeois society offers, instead of devoting himself to playing his own variation of 'Ain't It Awful'.

3 · RAPO

Thesis. This is a game played between a man and a woman which might more politely be called, in the milder forms at least, 'Kiss Off' or 'Indignation'. It may be played with varying degrees of intensity.

1. First-Degree 'Rapo', or 'Kiss Off', is popular at social gatherings and consists essentially of mild flirtation. White signals that she is available and gets her pleasure from the man's pursuit. As soon as he has committed himself, the game is over. If she is polite, she may say quite frankly 'I appreciate your compliments and thank you very much', and move on to the next conquest. If she is less generous, she may simply leave him. A skilful player can make this game last for a long time at a large social gathering by moving around frequently, so that the man has to carry out complicated manoeuvres in order to follow her without being too obvious.

2. In Second-Degree 'Rapo', or 'Indignation', White gets only secondary satisfaction from Black's advances. Her primary gratification comes from rejecting him, so that this game is also collo-

quially known as 'Buzz Off, Buster'. She leads Black into a much more serious commitment than the mild flirtation of First-Degree 'Rapo' and enjoys watching his discomfiture when she repulses him. Black, of course, is not as helpless as he seems, and may have gone to considerable trouble to get himself involved. Usually he is playing some variation of 'Kick Me'.

3. Third-Degree 'Rapo' is a vicious game which ends in murder, suicide or the courtroom. Here White leads Black into compromising physical contact and then claims that he has made a criminal assault or has done her irreparable damage. In its most cynical form White may actually allow him to complete the sexual act so that she gets that enjoyment before confronting him. The confrontation may be immediate, as in the illegitimate cry of rape, or it may be long delayed, as in suicide or homicide following a prolonged love affair. If she chooses to play it as a criminal assault, she may have no difficulty in finding mercenary or morbidly interested allies, such as the press, the police, counsellors and relatives. Sometimes, however, these outsiders may cynically turn on her, so that she loses the initiative and becomes a tool in their games.

In some cases outsiders perform a different function. They force the game on an unwilling White because they want to play 'Let's You and Him Fight'. They put her in such a position that in order to save her face or her reputation she has to cry rape. This is particularly apt to happen with girls under the legal age of consent; they may be quite willing to continue a liaison, but because it is discovered or made an issue of, they feel constrained to turn the romance into a game of Third-Degree 'Rapo'.

In one well-known situation, the wary Joseph refused to be inveigled into a game of 'Rapo', whereupon Potiphar's wife made the classical switch into 'Let's You and Him Fight', an excellent example of the way a hard player reacts to antithesis, and of the dangers that beset people who refuse to play games. These two games are combined in the well-known 'Badger Game', in which the woman seduces Black and then cries rape, at which point her husband takes charge and abuses Black for purposes of blackmail.

One of the most unfortunate and acute forms of Third-Degree 'Rapo' occurs relatively frequently between homosexual strangers, who in a matter of an hour or so may bring the game to a point of homicide. The cynical and criminal variations of this game contribute a large volume to sensational newspaper copy.

The childhood prototype of 'Rapo' is the same as that of 'Frigid Woman', in which the little girl induces the boy to humiliate himself or get dirty and then sneers at him, as classically described by Maugham in *Of Human Bondage* and, as already noted, by Dickens in *Great Expectations*. This is Second Degree. A harder form, approaching Third Degree, may be played in tough neighbourhoods.

Antithesis. The man's ability to avoid becoming involved in this game or to keep it under control depends on his capacity to distinguish genuine expressions of feeling from moves in the game. If he is thus able to exert social control, he may obtain a great deal of pleasure from the mild flirtations of 'Kiss Off'. On the other hand it is difficult to conceive of a safe antithesis for the Potiphar's Wife manoeuvre, other than checking out before closing time with no forwarding address. In 1938 the writer met an ageing Joseph in Aleppo who had checked out of Constantinople thirty-two years previously, after one of the Sultan's ladies had cornered him during a business visit to the Yildiz harem. He had to abandon his shop, but took time to pick up his hoard of gold francs, and had never returned.

Relatives. The male versions of 'Rapo' are notoriously found in commercial situations: 'Casting Couch' (and then she didn't get the part) and 'Cuddle Up' (and then she got fired).

ANALYSIS

The following analysis refers to Third-Degree 'Rapo' because there the elements of the game are more dramatically illustrated.

Aim: Malicious revenge.

Roles: Seductress, Wolf.

Dynamics (Third Degree): Penis envy, oral violence. 'Kiss Off' is phallic, while 'Indignation' has strong anal elements.

Examples: (1) I'll tell on you, you dirty little boy. (2) Wronged woman.

Social Paradigm: Adult-Adult.

Adult (male): 'I'm sorry if I went further than you intended me to.'

Adult (female): 'You have violated me and must pay the full penalty.'

Psychological Paradigm: Child-Child.

Child (male): 'See how irresistible I am.'

Child (female): 'Now I've got you, you son of a bitch.'

Moves: (1) Female: seduction; Male: counter-seduction. (2) Female: surrender; Male: victory. (3) Female: confrontation; Male: collapse.

Advantages: (1) Internal Psychological – expression of hatred and projection of guilt. (2) External Psychological – avoidance of emotional sexual intimacy. (3) Internal Social – 'Now I've Got You, You Son of a Bitch'. (4) External Social – 'Ain't It Awful', 'Courtroom', 'Let's You and Him Fight'. (5) Biological – sexual and belligerent exchanges. (6) Existential – I am blameless.

4 · THE STOCKING GAME

Thesis. This is a game of the 'Rapo' family; in it the most obvious characteristic is the exhibitionism, which is hysterical in nature. A woman comes into a strange group and after a very short time raises her leg, exposing herself in a provocative way, and remarks, 'Oh my, I have a run in my stocking.' This is calculated to arouse the men sexually and to make the other women angry. Any confrontation of White is met, of course, with protestations of innocence or counter-accusations, hence the resemblance to classical 'Rapo'. What is significant is White's lack of adaptation. She seldom waits to find out what kind of people she is dealing with or how to time her manoeuvre. Hence it stands out as inappropriate and affects her relationships with her associates. In spite of some superficial 'sophistication', she fails to understand what happens to her in life because her judgement of human nature is too cynical. The aim is to prove that other people have lascivious minds, and her Adult is conned by her Child and her Parent (usually a lascivious mother) into ignoring both her own provocativeness and the good sense of many of the people she meets. Thus the game tends to be self-destructive.

This is probably a phallic variant of a game whose content depends on the underlying disturbance. An 'oral' variant may be exhibited by women with deeper pathology and well-developed breasts. Such women often sit with their hands behind their heads so as to thrust their breasts forward; they may draw additional attention to them by remarking about their size or some pathology such as an operation or a lump. Some types of squirming probably constitute an anal variant. The implication of this game is that the woman is sexually available. Thus it may be played in a more symbolic form by bereaved women who 'exhibit' their widowhood insincerely.

Antithesis. Along with the poor adaptation, these women show little tolerance for antithesis. If the game is ignored or countered by a sophisticated therapy group, for example, they may not return. Antithesis must be carefully distinguished in this game from reprisal, since the latter signifies that White has won. Women are more skilful at counter-moves in 'Stocking Game' than men, who indeed have little incentive to break up this game. Antithesis, therefore, is best left to the discretion of the other women present.

5 · UPROAR

Thesis. The classical game is played between domineering fathers and teen-age daughters, where there is a sexually inhibited mother. Father comes home from work and finds fault with daughter, who answers impudently, or daughter may make the first move by being impudent, whereupon father finds fault. Their voices rise, and the clash becomes more acute. The outcome depends on who has the initiative. There are three possibilities: (*a*) father retires to his bedroom and slams the door; (*b*) daughter retires to her bedroom and slams the door; (*c*) both retire to their respective bedrooms and slam the doors. In any case, the end of a game of 'Uproar' is marked by a slamming door. 'Uproar' offers a distressing but effective solution to the sexual problems that arise between fathers and teen-age daughters in certain households. Often they can only live in the same house together if they are angry at each other, and the slamming doors emphasize for each of them the fact that they have separate bedrooms.

In degenerate households this game may be played in a sinister and repellent form in which father waits up for daughter whenever she goes out on a date, and examines her and her clothing carefully on her return to make sure that she has not had intercourse. The slightest suspicious circumstance may give rise to the most violent altercation, which may end with the daughter being expelled from the house in the middle of the night. In the long run nature will take its course – if not that night then the next, or the one after. Then the father's suspicions are 'justified', as he makes plain to the mother, who has stood by 'helplessly' while all this went on.

In general, however, 'Uproar' may be played between any two people who are trying to avoid sexual intimacy. For example, it is a common terminal phase of 'Frigid Woman'. It is relatively rare between teen-age boys and their female relatives, because it is easier for teen-age boys to escape from the house in the evening than for other members of the family. At an earlier age brothers and sisters can set up effective barriers and partial satisfactions through physical combat, a pattern which has various motivations at different ages, and which in America is a semi-ritualistic form of 'Uproar' sanctioned by television, pedagogic and pediatric authorities. In upper-class England it is (or was) considered bad form, and the corresponding energies are channelled into the well-regulated 'Uproar' of the playing fields.

Antithesis. The game is not as distasteful to the father as he might like to think, and it is generally the daughter who makes the antithetical move through an early, often premature or forced marriage. If it is psychologically possible, the mother can make the antithetical move by relinquishing her relative or absolute frigidity. The game may subside if the father finds an outside sexual interest, but that may lead to other complications. In the case of married couples, the antitheses are the same as for 'Frigid Woman' or 'Frigid Man'.

Under appropriate circumstances 'Uproar' leads quite naturally into 'Courtroom'.

10 · Underworld Games

WITH the infiltration of the 'helping' professions into the courts, probation departments and correctional facilities, and with the increasing sophistication of criminologists and law enforcement officers, those concerned should be aware of the more common games prevalent in the underworld, both in prison and out of it. These include 'Cops and Robbers', 'How Do You Get Out of Here' and 'Let's Pull a Fast One on Joey'.

1 · COPS AND ROBBERS

Thesis. Because many criminals are cop-haters, they seem to get as much satisfaction from outwitting the police as from their criminal gains, often more. Their crimes, at the Adult level, are games played for the material rewards, the take; but at the Child level it is the thrill of the chase: the getaway and the cool-off.

Curiously enough, the childhood prototype of 'Cops and Robbers' is not cops and robbers but hide-and-seek, in which the essential element is the chagrin at being found. Younger children readily betray this. If father finds them too easily, the chagrin is there without much fun. But father, if he is a good player, knows what to do: he holds off, whereupon the little boy gives him a clue by calling out, dropping something or banging. Thus he forces father to find him, but still shows chagrin; this time he has had more fun because of the increased suspense. If father gives up, the boy usually feels disappointed rather than victorious. Since the fun of being hidden was there, evidently that is not where the trouble lies. What he is disappointed about is not being caught. When his turn comes to hide, father knows he is not supposed to outwit the little boy for very long, just long enough to make it fun; and he is wise enough to look chagrined when he is caught. It soon becomes clear that being found is the necessary payoff.

Hence hide-and-seek is not a mere pastime but a true game. At the social level it is a battle of wits, and is most satisfying when the Adult of each player does his best; at the psychological level, however, it is set up like compulsive gambling, in which White's Adult has to lose in order for his Child to win. Not being caught is actually the antithesis. Among older children, one who finds an insoluble hiding place is regarded as not being a good sport, since he has spoiled the game. He has eliminated the Child element and turned the whole thing into an Adult procedure. He is no longer playing for fun. He is in the same class as the owner of a casino, or some professional criminals, who are really out for money rather than sport.

There seem to be two distinctive types of habitual criminals: those who are in crime primarily for profit, and those who are in it primarily for the game – with a large group in between who can handle it either way. The 'compulsive winner', the big money-maker whose Child really does not want to be caught, rarely is, according to reports; he is an untouchable, for whom the fix is always in. The 'compulsive loser', on the other hand, who is playing 'Cops and Robbers' (C & R), seldom does very well financially. The exceptions to this often seem to be due to luck rather than skill; in the long run even the lucky ones usually end up as their Child requires, squawking rather than riding high.

The C & R player, with whom we are concerned here, in some ways resembles the Alcoholic. He can shift roles from Robber to Cop and from Cop to Robber. In some cases he may play the Parental Cop during the day and the Child Robber after dark. There is a Cop in many Robbers, and a Robber in many Cops. If the criminal 'reforms', he may play the role of Rescuer, becoming a social worker or a mission worker; but the Rescuer is far less important in this game than in 'Alcoholic'. Ordinarily, however, the player's role as Robber is his destiny, and each has his own *modus operandi* for getting caught. He may make it tough or easy for the Cops.

The situation is similar with gamblers. At the social or sociological level a 'professional' gambler is one whose chief interest in life is gambling. But at the psychological level there are two different kinds of people who are professional gamblers. There are those who spend their time gaming, i.e., playing with Fate, in whom the strength of the Adult's desire to win is exceeded only by the strength of the Child's need to lose. Then there are those who run gambling houses and actually do earn a living, usually a very good one, by providing opportunities for gamesters to play; they themselves are not playing, and try to avoid playing, although occasionally under certain conditions they will indulge themselves and enjoy it, just as a straight criminal may occasionally play a game of C & R.

This throws light on why sociological and psychological studies of criminals have been generally ambiguous and unproductive: they are dealing with two different kinds of people who cannot be adequately differentiated in the ordinary theoretical or empirical frameworks. The same is true in studying gamblers. Transactional and game analyses offer an immediate solution for this. They remove the ambiguity by distinguishing transactionally, below the social level, between 'players' and 'straight professionals'.

Let us now turn from this general thesis to consider specific examples. Some burglars do their jobs without any waste motion. The 'Cops and Robbers' burglar leaves his calling card in gratuitous acts of vandalism, such as spoiling valuable clothing with secretions and excretions. The straight bank robber, according to reports, takes every possible precaution to avoid violence; the C & R bank robber is only looking for an excuse to vent his anger. Like any professional, a straight criminal likes his jobs to be as clean as circumstances permit. The C & R criminal is compelled to blow off steam in the course of his work. The true professional is said never to operate until the fix is in; the player is willing to take on the law barehanded. Straight professionals are well aware, in their own way, of the game of C & R. If a gang member shows too much interest in the game, to the point of jeopardizing the job, and particularly if his need to be caught begins to show, they will take drastic measures to prevent a recurrence. Perhaps it is just because straight professionals are not playing C & R that they are so seldom caught, and hence so rarely studied sociologically, psychologically and psychiatrically; and this also applies to gamblers. Hence most of our clinical knowledge about criminals and gamblers refers to players rather than to straight professionals.

Kleptomaniacs (as opposed to professional shoplifters) are examples of how widely trivial C & R is played. It is probable that a very large percentage of Occidentals, at least, have played C & R in fantasy, and that is what sells newspapers in our half of the world. This fantasy frequently occurs in the form of dreaming up the 'perfect murder', which is playing the hardest possible game and completely outwitting the cops.

Variations of C & R are 'Auditors and Robbers', played by embezzlers with the same rules and the same payoff; 'Customs and Robbers', played by smugglers, etc. Of special interest is the criminal variation of 'Courtroom'. Despite all his precautions, the professional may occasionally be arrested and brought to trial. For him 'Courtroom' is a procedure, which he carries out according to the instructions of his legal advisers. For the lawyers, if they are compulsive winners, 'Courtroom' is essentially a game played with the jury in which the object is to win, not lose, and this is regarded as a constructive game by a large segment of society.

Antithesis. This is the concern of qualified criminologists rather than psychiatrists. The police and judiciary apparatus are not antithetical, but are playing their roles in the game under the rules set up by society.

One thing should be emphasized, however. Research workers in criminology may joke that some criminals behave as though they enjoyed the chase and wanted to be caught, or they may read the idea and agree in a deferential way. But they show little tendency to consider such an 'academic' factor as decisive in their 'serious' work. For one thing, there is no way to unmask this element through the standard methods of psychological research. The investigator must therefore either overlook a crucial point because he cannot work it with his research tools, or else change his tools. The fact is that those tools have so far not yielded one single solution to any problem in criminology. Researchers might therefore be better off discarding the old methods and tackling the problem freshly. Until C & R is accepted not merely as an interesting anomaly, but as the very heart of the matter in a significant percentage of cases, much research in criminology will continue to deal with trivialities, doctrines, peripheral issues or irrelevancies.[1]

ANALYSIS

Thesis: See if you can catch me.

Aim: Reassurance.

Roles: Robber, Cop (Judge).

Dynamics: Phallic intrusion, e.g., (1) Hide-and-seek, tag.

(2) Crime.

   Social Paradigm: Parent-Child.

      Child: 'See if you can catch me.'

      Parent: 'That's my job.'

   Psychological Paradigm: Parent-Child.

      Child: 'You must catch me.'

      Parent: 'Aha, there you are.'

   Moves: (1) W: Defiance. B: Indignation. (2) W: Concealment. B: Frustration. (3) W: Provocation. B: Victory.

   Advantages: (1) Internal Psychological – material indemnification for old wrong. (2) External Psychological – counterphobic. (3) Internal Social– See if you can catch me. (4) External Social – I almost got away with it (Pastime: They almost got away with it.) (5) Biological – notoriety. (6) Existential: I've always been a loser.

2 · HOW DO YOU GET OUT OF HERE

Thesis. The historical evidence is that those prisoners survive best who have their time structured by an activity, pastime or a game. This is apparently well known to political police, who are said to break some prisoners down simply by keeping them inactive and in a state of social deprivation.

The favoured *activity* of solitary prisoners is reading or writing books, and the favoured *pastime* is escape, some of whose practitioners, such as Casanova and Baron Trenck, have become famous.

The favoured *game* is 'How Do You Get Out of Here?' ('Want Out'), which may also be played in state hospitals. It must be distinguished from the *operation* (see page 44) of the same name, known as 'Good Behaviour'. An inmate who really wants to be free will find out how to comply with the authorities so as to be released at the earliest possible moment. Nowadays this may often be accomplished by playing a good game of 'Psychiatry', Group Therapy Type. The game of 'Want Out', however, is played by inmates or by patients whose Child does *not* want to get out. They simulate 'Good Behaviour', but at the critical point they sabotage themselves so as not to be released. Thus in 'Good Behaviour' Parent, Adult and Child work together to be discharged; in 'Want Out' Parent and Adult go through the prescribed motions until the critical moment, when the Child, who is actually frightened at the prospect of venturing into the uncertain world, takes over and spoils the effect. 'Want Out' was common in the late 1930s among recently arrived immigrants from Germany who became psychotic. They would improve and beg for release from the hospital; but as the day of liberation approached, their psychotic manifestations would recur.

Antithesis. Both 'Good Behaviour' and 'Want Out' are recognized by alert administrators and can be dealt with at the executive level. Beginners in group therapy, however, are often taken in. A competent group therapist, knowing these are the most frequent manipulations in psychiatrically oriented prisons, will be watching for them and will ferret them out at an early phase. Since 'Good Behaviour' is an honest operation, it may be treated as such, and there is no harm in discussing it openly. 'Want Out', on the other hand, requires active therapy if the frightened inmate is to be rehabilitated.

Relatives. A close relative of 'Want Out' is an operation called 'You've Got to Listen'. Here the inmate of an institution or the client of a social agency demands the right to make complaints. The complaints are often irrelevant. His main purpose is to assure himself that he will be listened to by the authorities. If they make the mistake of thinking that he expects the complaints to be acted on and cut him off as too demanding, there may be trouble. If they accede to his demands, he will increase them. If they merely listen patiently and with signs of interest, the 'You've Got to Listen' player will be satisfied and cooperative, and will not ask for anything more. The administrator must learn to distinguish 'You've Got to Listen' from serious demands for remedial action.[2]

'Bum Rap' is another game that belongs in this family. A straight criminal may holler 'Bum Rap' in a real effort to get out, in which case it is part of the procedure. The inmate who plays 'Bum Rap' as a game, however, does not use it effectively to try to get out, since if he gets out he will no longer have much excuse to holler.

3 · LET'S PULL A FAST ONE ON JOEY

Thesis. The prototype of this game is 'The Big Store', the big-time confidence game, but many small grifts and even the badger game are FOOJY. No man can be beaten at FOOJY unless he has larceny in his veins, because the first move is for Black to tell White that dumb-honest-old-Joey is just waiting to be taken. If White were completely honest, he would either back off or warn Joey, but he doesn't. Just as Joey is about to pay off, something goes wrong, and White finds that his investment is gone. Or in the badger game, just as Joey is about to be cuckolded, he happens to walk in. Then White, who was playing his own rules in his own honest way, finds that he has to play Joey's rules, and they hurt.

Curiously enough, the mark is supposed to know the rules of FOOJY and stick to them. Honest squawking is a calculated risk of the con mob; they will not hold that against White, and he is even allowed a certain latitude in lying to the police to save his face. But if he goes too far and accuses them falsely of burglary, for example, that is cheating, and they resent it. On the other hand, there is little sympathy for a con man who gets into trouble by working a mark who is drunk, since this is improper procedure, and he should know better. The same applies if he is stupid enough to pick a mark with a sense of humour, since it is well known that such people cannot be trusted to play the straight man in FOOJY all the way down the line through the terminal game of 'Cops and Robbers'. Experienced con men are scared of marks who laugh after they have been taken.

It should be noted that a practical joke is not a game of FOOJY, because in a practical joke Joey is the one who suffers, while in FOOJY Joey comes out on top, and White is the one who suffers. A practical joke is a pastime, while FOOJY is a game in which the joke is arranged to backfire.

It is evident that FOOJY is a three- or four-handed game, with the police playing the fourth hand, and that it is related to 'Let's You and Him Fight'.

NOTE

Thanks are due to Dr Franklin Ernst of the California Medical Faculty at Vacaville, Mr William Collins of the California Rehabilitation Center at Norco, and Mr Laurence Means of the California Institution for Men at Tehachapi, for their continued interest in studying the game of 'Cops and Robbers' and for their helpful discussions and criticisms.

REFERENCES

1. Frederick Wiseman, in 'Psychiatry and the Law: Use and Abuse of Psychiatry in a Murder Case' (*American Journal of Psychiatry*, 118: 289–299, 1961) gives a clear and tragic example of a hard form of 'Cops and Robbers'. It concerns a 23-year-old-man who shot his fiancée and then turned himself in. This was not easy to arrange, since the police did not believe his story until he had repeated it four times. Later, he said: 'It just seemed to me that all my life I was bound to end up in the chair. If that was the way it was, that was the way it would be.' The author says it was farcical to expect a lay jury to understand the complex psychiatric testimony that was offered at the trial in technical jargon. In game terms, the central issue can be stated in words of no more than two syllables: A nine-year-old boy decides (for reasons clearly brought out at the trial) that he is bound to end up in the chair. He spends the rest of his life headed toward this goal, and using his girl friend as a target, in the end he sets himself up.

2. For further information about 'Cops and Robbers' and games played by prison inmates, see: Ernst, F. H., and Keating, W. C., 'Psychiatric Treatment of the California Felon', *American Journal of Psychiatry*, 120: 974–979, 1964.

11 · Consulting Room Games

GAMES that are tenaciously played in the therapeutic situation are the most important ones for the professional game analyst to be aware of. They can be most readily studied first hand in the consulting room. There are three types, according to the role of the agent:

1. Games played by therapists and case workers: 'I'm Only Trying to Help You' and 'Psychiatry'.

2. Games played by professionally trained people who are patients in therapy groups, such as 'Greenhouse'.

3. Games played by lay patients and clients: 'Indigent', 'Peasant', 'Stupid' and 'Wooden Leg'.

1 · GREENHOUSE

Thesis. This is a variation of 'Psychiatry', which is played hardest by young social scientists, such as clinical psychologists. In the company of their colleagues these young people tend to play 'Psychoanalysis', often in a jocular way, using such expressions as 'Your hostility is showing' or 'How mechanical can a defence mechanism get?' This is usually a harmless and enjoyable pastime; it is a normal phase of their learning experience, and with a few originals in the group it can become quite amusing. (This writer's preference is, 'I see National Parapraxis Week is here again.') As patients in psychotherapy groups some of these people are apt to indulge in this mutual critique more seriously; but since it is not highly productive in that situation, it may have to be headed off by the therapist. The proceedings may then turn into a game of 'Greenhouse'.

There is a strong tendency for recent graduates to have an exaggerated respect for what they call 'Genuine Feelings'. The expression of such a feeling may be preceded by an announcement that it is on its way. After the announcement, the feeling is described, or rather presented before the group, as though it were a rare flower which should be regarded with awe. The reactions of the other members are received very solemnly, and they take on the air of connoisseurs at a botanical garden. The problem seems to be, in the jargon of game analysis, whether this one is good enough to be exhibited in the National Feeling Show. A questioning intervention by the therapist may be strongly resented, as though he were some clumsy-fingered clod mauling the fragile petals of an exotic century plant. The therapist, naturally, feels that in order to understand the anatomy and physiology of a flower, it may be necessary to dissect it.

Antithesis. The antithesis, which is crucial for therapeutic progress, is the irony of the above description. If this game is allowed to proceed, it may go on unchanged for years, after which the patient may feel that he has had a 'therapeutic experience' during which he has 'expressed hostility' and learned to 'face feelings' in a way which gives him an advantage over less fortunate colleagues. Meanwhile very little of dynamic significance may have happened, and certainly the investment of time has not been used to maximum therapeutic advantage.

The irony in the initial description is directed not against the patients but against their teachers and the cultural milieu which encourages such over-fastidiousness. If properly timed, a sceptical remark may successfully divorce them from foppish Parental influences and lead to a less self-conscious robustness in their transactions with each other. Instead of cultivating feelings in a kind of hothouse atmosphere, they may just let them grow naturally, to be plucked when they are ripe.

The most obvious advantage of this game is the external psychological, since it avoids intimacy by setting up special conditions under which feelings may be expressed, and special restrictions on the responses of those present.

2 · I'M ONLY TRYING TO HELP YOU

Thesis. This game may be played in any professional situation and is not confined to psychotherapists and welfare workers. However, it is found most commonly and in its most florid form among social workers with a certain type of training. The analysis of this game was clarified for the writer under curious circumstances. All the players at a poker game had folded except two, a research psychologist and a businessman. The businessman, who had a high hand, bet; the psychologist, who had an unbeatable one, raised. The businessman looked puzzled, whereupon the psychologist remarked facetiously: 'Don't be upset, I'm only trying to help you!' The businessman hesitated, and finally put in his chips. The psychologist showed the winning hand, whereupon the other threw down his cards in disgust. The others present then felt free to laugh at the psychologist's joke, and the loser remarked ruefully: 'You sure were helpful!' The psychologist cast a knowing glance at the writer, implying that the joke had really been made at the expense of the psychiatric profession. It was at that moment that the structure of this game became clear.

The worker or therapist, of whatever profession, gives some advice to a client or patient. The patient returns and reports that the suggestion did not have the desired effect. The worker shrugs off this failure with a feeling of resignation, and tries again. If he is more watchful, he may detect at this point a twinge of frustration, but he will try again anyway. Usually he feels little need to question his own motives, because he knows that many of his similarly trained colleagues do the same thing, and that he is following the 'correct' procedure and will receive full support from his supervisors.

If he runs up against a hard player, such as a hostile obsessional, he will find it more and more difficult to avoid feeling inadequate. Then he is in trouble, and the situation will slowly deteriorate. In the worst case, he may come up against an angry paranoid who will rush in one day in a rage, crying:'Look what you made me do!' Then his frustration will come strongly to the fore in the spoken or unspoken thought: 'But I was only trying to help you!' His bewilderment at the ingratitude may cause him considerable suffering, indicating the complex motives underlying his own behaviour. This bewilderment is the payoff.

Legitimate helpers should not be confused with people who play 'I'm Only Trying to Help You' (ITHY). 'I think we can do something about it', 'I know what to do', 'I was assigned to help you' or 'My fee for helping you will be . .' are different from 'I'm only trying to help you'. The first four, in good faith, represent Adult offers to put professional qualifications at the disposal of the distressed patient or client; ITHY has an ulterior motive which is more important than professional skill in determining the outcome. This motive is based on the position that people are ungrateful and disappointing. The prospect of success is alarming to the Parent of the professional and is an invitation to sabotage, because success would threaten the position. The ITHY player needs to be reassured that help will not be accepted no matter how strenuously it is offered. The client responds with 'Look How Hard I'm Trying' or 'There's Nothing You Can Do to Help Me'. More flexible players can compromise: it is all right for people to accept help providing it takes them a long time to do so. Hence therapists tend to feel apologetic for a quick result, since they know that some of their colleagues at staff meetings will be critical. At the opposite pole from hard ITHY players, such as are found among social workers, are good lawyers who help their clients without personal involvement or sentimentality. Here craftsmanship takes the place of covert strenuousness.

Some schools of social work seem to be primarily academies for the training of professional ITHY players, and it is not easy for their graduates to desist from playing it. An example which may help to illustrate some of the foregoing points will be found in the description of the complementary game 'Indigence'.

ITHY and its variants are easy to find in everyday life. It is played by family friends and relatives (e.g., 'I Can Get It For You Wholesale'), and by adults who do community work with children. It is a favourite among parents, and the complementary game played by the offspring is usually 'Look What You Made Me Do'. Socially it may be a variant of 'Schlemiel' in which the damage is done while being helpful rather than impulsively; here the client is represented by a victim who may be playing 'Why Does This Always Happen To Me?' or one of its variants.

Antithesis. There are several devices available for the professional to handle an invitation to play this game, and his selection will depend on the state of the relationship between himself and the patient, particularly on the attitude of the patient's Child.

1. The classical psychoanalytic antithesis is the most thoroughgoing and the most difficult for the patient to tolerate. The invitation is completely ignored. The patient then tries harder and harder. Eventually he falls into a state of despair, manifested by anger or depression, which is the characteristic sign that a game has been frustrated. This situation may lead to a useful confrontation.

2. A more gentle (but not prim) confrontation may be attempted on the first invitation. The therapist states that he is the patient's therapist and not his manager.

3. An even more gentle procedure is to introduce the patient into a therapy group, and let the other patients handle it.

4. With an acutely disturbed patient it may be necessary to play along during the initial phase. These patients should be treated by a psychiatrist, who being a medical man, can prescribe both medications and some of the hygienic measures which are still valuable, even in this day of tranquillizers, in the treatment of such people. If the physician prescribes a hygienic regimen, which may include baths, exercise, rest periods, and regular meals along with medication, the patient (1) carries out the regimen and feels better (2) carries out the regimen scrupulously and complains that it does not help; (3) mentions casually that he forgot to carry out the instructions or that he has abandoned the regimen because it was not doing any good. In the second and third case it is then up to the psychiatrist to decide whether the patient is amenable to game analysis at that point, or whether some other form of treatment is indicated to prepare him for later psychotherapy. The relationship between the adequacy of the regimen and the patient's tendency to play games with it should be carefully evaluated by the psychiatrist before he decides how to proceed next.

For the patient, on the other hand, the antithesis is, 'Don't tell me what to do to help myself, I'll tell you what to do to help me.' If the therapist is known to be a Schlemiel, the correct antithesis for the patient to use is, 'Don't help me, help him.' But serious players of 'I'm Only Trying to Help You' are generally lacking in a sense of humour. Antithetical moves on the part of a patient are usually unfavourably received, and may result in the therapist's lifelong enmity. In everyday life such moves should not be initiated unless one is prepared to carry them through ruthlessly and take the consequences. For example, spurning a relative who 'Can Get It For You Wholesale' may cause serious domestic complications.

ANALYSIS

Thesis: Nobody ever does what I tell them.
Aim: Alleviation of guilt.

Roles: Helper, Client.

Dynamics: Masochism.

Examples: (1) Children learning, parent intervenes. (2) Social worker and client.

Social Paradigm: Parent-Child.

Child: 'What do I do now?'

Parent: 'Here's what you do.'

Psychological Paradigm: Parent-Child.

Parent: 'See how adequate I am.'

Child: 'I'll make you feel inadequate.'

Moves: (1) Instructions requested – Instructions given. (2) Procedure bungled – Reproof. (3) Demonstration that procedures are faulty – Implicit apology.

Advantages: (1) Internal Psychological – martyrdom. (2) External Psychological – avoids facing inadequacies. (3) Internal Social – 'PTA', Projective Type; ingratitude. (4) External Social – 'Psychiatry', Projective Type. (5) Biological – slapping from client, stroking from supervisors. (6) Existential – All people are ungrateful.

3 · INDIGENCE

Thesis. The thesis of this game is best stated by Henry Miller in *The Colossus of Maroussi:* 'The event must have taken place during the year when I was looking for a job without the slightest intention of taking one. It reminded me that, desperate as I thought myself to be, I had not even bothered to look through the columns of the want ads.'

This game is one of the complements of 'I'm Only Trying to Help You' (ITHY) as it is played by social workers who earn their living by it. 'Indigence' is played just as professionally by the client who earns his living in this manner. The writer's own experience with 'Indigence' is limited, but the following account by one of his most accomplished students illustrates the nature of this game and its place in our society.

Miss Black was a social worker in a welfare agency whose avowed purpose, for which it received a government subsidy, was the economic rehabilitation of indigents – which in effect meant getting them to find and retain gainful employment. The clients of this agency were continually 'making progress', according to official reports, but very few of them were actually 'rehabilitated'. This was understandable, it was claimed, because most of them had been welfare clients for several years, going from agency to agency and sometimes being involved with five or six agencies at a time, so that it was evident that they were 'difficult cases'.

Miss Black, from her training in game analysis, soon realized that the staff of her agency was playing a consistent game of ITHY, and wondered how the clients were responding to this. In order to check, she asked her own clients from week to week how many job opportunities they had actually investigated. She was interested to discover that although they were theoretically supposed to be looking assiduously for work from day to day, actually they devoted very little effort to this, and sometimes the token efforts they did make had an ironic quality. For example, one man said that he answered at least one advertisement a day looking for work. 'What kind of work?' she inquired. He said he wanted to go into saleswork. 'Is that the only kind of ad you answer?' she asked. He said that it was, but it was too bad that he was a stutterer, as that held him back from his chosen career. About this time it came to the attention of her supervisor that she was asking these questions, and she was reprimanded for putting 'undue pressure' on her clients.

Miss Black decided nevertheless to go ahead and rehabilitate some of them. She selected those who were able-bodied and did not seem to have a valid reason to continue to receive welfare funds. With this selected group, she talked over the games ITHY and 'Indigence'. When they were willing to concede the point, she said that unless they found jobs she was going to cut them off from welfare funds and refer them to a different kind of agency. Several of them almost immediately found employment, some for the first time in years. But they were indignant at her attitude, and some of them wrote letters to her supervisor complaining about it. The supervisor called her in and reprimanded her even more severely on the ground that although her former clients were working, they were not 'really rehabilitated'. The supervisor indicated that there was some question whether they would retain Miss Black in the agency. Miss Black, as much as she dared without further jeopardizing her position, tactfully tried to elicit what would constitute

'really rehabilitated' in the agency's opinion. This was not clarified. She was only told that she was 'putting undue pressure' on
people, and the fact that they were supporting their families for the
first time in years was in no way to her credit.

Because she needed her job and was now in danger of losing it,
some of her friends tried to help. The respected head of a psychiatric clinic wrote to the supervisor, stating that he had heard
Miss Black had done some particularly effective work with
welfare clients, and asking whether she might discuss her findings at a staff conference at his clinic. The supervisor refused
permission.

In this case the rules of 'Indigent' were set up by the agency to
complement the local rules of ITHY. There was a tacit agreement
between the worker and the client which read as follows:

> W. 'I'll try to help you (providing you don't get better).'
> C. 'I'll look for employment (providing I don't have to find any).

If a client broke the agreement by getting better, the agency lost
a client, and the client lost his welfare benefits, and both felt
penalized. If a worker like Miss Black broke the agreement by
making the client actually find work, the agency was penalized by
the client's complaints, which might come to the attention of
higher authorities, while again the client lost his welfare benefits.

As long as both obeyed the implicit rules, both got what they
wanted. The client received his benefits and soon learned what
the agency wanted in return: an opportunity to 'reach out' (as
part of ITHY) plus 'clinical material' (to present at 'client-
centred' staff conferences). The client was glad to comply with
these demands, which gave him as much pleasure as it did the agency. Thus they got along well together, and neither felt any desire
to terminate such a satisfying relationship. Miss Black, in effect,
'reached in' instead of 'reaching out', and proposed a 'commu-
nity-centred' staff conference instead of a 'client-centred' one; and
this disturbed all the others concerned in spite of the fact that she
was thus only complying with the stated intent of the regulations.

Two things should be noted here. First, 'Indigence' as a game
rather than a condition due to physical, mental, or economic
disability, is played by only a limited percentage of welfare clients.
Second, it will only be supported by social workers who are

trained to play ITHY. It will not be well-tolerated by other workers.

Allied games are 'Veteran' and 'Clinic'. 'Veteran' displays the same symbiotic relationship, this time between the Veterans Administration, allied organizations, and a certain number of 'professional veterans' who share the legitimate privileges of disabled ex-servicemen. 'Clinic' is played by a certain percentage of those who attend the out-patient departments of large hospitals. Unlike those who play 'Indigent' or 'Veteran', patients who play 'Clinic' do not receive financial remuneration, but get other advantages. They serve a useful social purpose, since they are willing to cooperate in the training of medical personnel and in studies of disease processes. From this they may get a legitimate Adult satisfaction not available to players of 'Indigence' and 'Veteran'.

Antithesis. Antithesis, if indicated, consists in withholding the benefits. Here the risk is not primarily from the player himself, as in most other games, but from this game being culturally syntonic and fostered by the complementary ITHY players. The threat comes from professional colleagues and the aroused public, government agencies and protective unions. The complaints which follow an exhibition of anti-'Indigence' may lead to a loud outcry of 'Yes, Yes, How About That?' which may be regarded as a healthy, constructive operation or pastime, even if it occasionally discourages candidness. In fact, the whole American political system of democratic freedoms is based on a licence (not available under many other forms of government) to ask that question. Without such a licence, humanitarian social progress becomes seriously impeded.

4 · PEASANT

Thesis. The prototype peasant is the arthritic Bulgarian villager who sells her only cow to raise money to go to the university clinic in Sofia. There the professor examines her and finds her case so interesting that he presents her in a clinical demonstration to the medical students. He outlines not only the pathology, symptoms and diagnosis, but also the treatment. This procedure fills her with awe. Before she leaves, the professor gives her a prescription and explains the treatment in more detail. She is overcome with admiration for his learning and says the Bulgarian equivalent of, 'Gee, you're wonderful, Professor!' However, she never has the prescription filled. First, there is no apothecary in her village; second, even if there were, she would never let such a valuable piece of paper out of her hands. Nor does she have the facilities for carrying out the rest of the treatment, such as diet, hydrotherapy and so on. She lives on, crippled as before, but happy now because she can tell everyone about the wonderful treatment prescribed for her by the great professor in Sofia, to whom she expresses her gratitude every night in her prayers.

Years later, the Professor, in an unhappy frame of mind, happens to pass through the village on his way to see a wealthy but demanding patient. He remembers the peasant when she rushes out to kiss his hand and remind him of the marvellous regimen he put her on so long ago. He accepts her homage graciously, and is particularly gratified when she tells him how much good the treatment has done. In fact he is so carried away that he fails to notice that she limps as badly as ever.

Socially 'Peasant' is played in an innocent and a dissembled form, both with the motto, 'Gee you're wonderful, Mr Murgatroyd!' (GYWM). In the innocent form, Murgatroyd *is* wonderful. He is a celebrated poet, painter, philanthropist or scientist, and naïve young women frequently travel a long way in the hope of meeting him so that they can sit adoringly at his feet and romanticize his imperfections. A more sophisticated woman who sets out deliberately to have an affair or a marriage with such a man, whom she sincerely admires and appreciates, may be fully aware of his weaknesses. She may even exploit them in order to get what she wants. With these two types of women, the game arises from the romanticizing or exploiting of the imperfections, while the innocence lies in their genuine respect for his accomplishments, which they are able to evaluate correctly.

In the dissembled form, Murgatroyd may or may not be wonderful, but he comes up against a woman incapable of appreciating him in the best sense, in any case; perhaps she is a high-class prostitute. She plays 'Little Old Me' and uses GYWM as sheer flattery to attain her own ends. Underneath she is either bewildered by him or laughing at him. But she does not care about him; what she wants are the perquisites that go with him.

Clinically 'Peasant' is played in two similar forms, with the motto, 'Gee you're wonderful, Professor!' (GYWP). In the innocent form the patient may stay well as long as she can believe in GYWP, which places an obligation on the therapist to be well-behaved both in public and in private life. In the dissembled form the patient hopes the therapist will go along with her GYWP and think: 'You're uncommonly perceptive.' (YUP). Once she has him in this position, she can make him look foolish and then move on to another therapist; if he cannot be so easily beguiled, he may actually be able to help her.

The simplest way for the patient to win GYWP is not to get better. If she is more malicious, she may take more positive steps to make the therapist look foolish. One woman played GYWP with her psychiatrist without any alleviations of symptoms; she finally left him with many salaams and apologies. She then went to her revered clergyman for help and played GYWP with him. After a few weeks she seduced him into a game of second degree 'Rapo'. She then told her neighbour confidentially over the back fence how disappointed she was that so fine a man as Rev Black could, in a moment of weakness, make a pass at an innocent and unattractive woman like herself. Knowing his wife, she could forgive him, of course, but nevertheless, etc. This confidence just slipped out inadvertently, and it was only afterwards that she remembered 'to her horror' that the neighbour was an elder in the church. With her psychiatrist she won by not getting better; with her clergyman she won by seducing him, although she was reluctant to admit it. But a second psychiatrist introduced her to a therapy group where she could not manoeuvre as she had before. Then, with no GYWP and YUP to fill in her therapeutic time, she began to examine her behaviour more closely and with the help of the group was able to give up both her games – GYWP and 'Rapo'.

Antithesis. The therapist must first decide whether the game is played innocently and hence should be allowed to continue for the benefit of the patient until her Adult is sufficiently well-established to risk countermeasures. If it is not innocent, the countermeasures may be taken at the first appropriate opportunity after the patient has been sufficiently well prepared so that she will be able to understand what happens. The therapist then steadfastly refuses to give advice, and when the patient begins to protest, he makes it clear that this is not merely 'Poker-Faced Psychiatry' but a well-thought-out policy. In due time his refusal may either enrage the patient or precipitate acute anxiety symptoms. The next step depends on the malignancy of the patient's condition. If she is too upset, her acute reactions should be dealt with by appropriate psychiatric or analy-tic procedures to re-establish the therapeutic situation. The first goal, in the dissembled form, is to split off the Adult from the hypocritical Child so that the game can be analysed.

In social situations, intimate entanglements with innocent GYWM players should be avoided, as any intelligent actor's agent will impress upon his clients. On the other hand, women who play dissembled GYWM are sometimes interesting and intelligent if they can be de-GYWMed, and may turn out to be quite a delightful addition to the family social circle.

5 · PSYCHIATRY

Thesis. Psychiatry as a procedure must be distinguished from 'Psychiatry' as a game. According to the available evidence, presented in proper clinical form in scientific publications, the following approaches, among others, are of value in treating psychiatric conditions: shock therapy, hypnosis, drugs, psycho-analysis, orthopsychiatry and group therapy. There are others which are less commonly used and will not be discussed here. Any of these can be used in the game of 'Psychiatry', which is based on the position 'I am a healer', supported by a diploma: 'It says here I am a healer'. It will be noted that in any case this is a constructive, benevolent position, and that people who play 'Psychiatry' can do a great deal of good, providing they are professionally trained.

It is likely, however, that there will be some gain in therapeutic results if therapeutic ardour is moderated. The *antithesis* was best expressed long ago by Ambroise Paré, who said in effect: 'I treat them, but God cures them.' Every medical student learns about this dictum, along with others such as *primum non nocere*, and phrases such as *vis medicatrix naturae*. Nonmedical therapists, however, are not so likely to be exposed to these ancient cautions. The position 'I am a healer because it says here that I am a healer' is likely to be an impairment, and may be replaced to advantage with something like: 'I will apply what therapeutic procedures I have learned in the hope that they will be of some benefit.' This avoids the possibility of games based on: 'Since I am a healer, if you don't get better it's your fault' (e.g., 'I'm Only Trying To Help You'), or 'Since you're a healer, I'll get better for you' (e.g., 'Peasant'). All of this, of course, is known in principle to every conscientious therapist. Certainly every therapist who has ever presented a case at a reputable clinic has been made aware of it. Conversely, a good clinic may be defined as one which makes its therapists aware of these things.

On the other side, the game of 'Psychiatry' is more apt to crop up with patients who have previously been treated by less competent therapists. A few patients, for example, carefully pick weak psychoanalysts, moving from one to another, demonstrating that they cannot be cured and meanwhile learning to play a sharper and sharper game of 'Psychiatry'; eventually it becomes difficult for even a first-rate clinician to separate the wheat from the chaff. The duplex transaction on the patient's side is:

Adult: 'I am coming to be cured.'
Child: 'You will never cure me, but you will teach me to be a better neurotic (play a better game of "Psychiatry").'

'Mental Health' is played similarly; here the Adult statement is, 'Everything will get better if I apply the principles of mental health which I have read and heard about.' One patient learned to play 'Psychiatry' from one therapist, 'Mental Health' from another, and then as a result of still another effort began to play a pretty good game of 'Transactional Analysis'. When this was frankly discussed with her, she agreed to stop playing 'Mental Health', but requested that she be allowed to continue to play 'Psychiatry' because it made her feel comfortable. The transactional psychiatrist agreed. She continued therefore for several months to recite her dreams and her interpretations of them at weekly intervals. Finally, partly out of plain gratitude, perhaps, she decided that it might be interesting to find out what was really the matter with her. She became seriously interested in transactional analysis, with good results.

A variant of 'Psychiatry' is 'Archaeology' (title by courtesy of Dr Norman Reider of San Francisco), in which the patient takes the position that if she can only find out who had the button, so to speak, everything will suddenly be all right. This results in a continual rumination over childhood happenings. Sometimes the therapist may be beguiled into a game of 'Critique', in which the patient describes her feelings in various situations and the therapist tells her what is wrong with them. 'Self-Expression', which is a common game in some therapy groups, is based on the dogma 'Feelings are Good'. A patient who uses vulgar expletives, for example, may be applauded or at least implicitly lauded. A sophisticated group, however, will soon spot this as a game.

Some members of therapy groups become quite adept at picking out games of 'Psychiatry', and will soon let a new patient know if they think he is playing 'Psychiatry' or 'Transactional Analysis' instead of using group procedures to obtain legitimate insight. A woman who transferred from a Self-Expression group in one city to a more sophisticated group in another city told a story about an incestuous relationship in her childhood. Instead of the awe which she had come to expect whenever she told this oft-repeated tale, she was greeted with indifference, whereupon she became enraged. She was astonished to discover that the new group was more interested in her transactional anger than in her historical incest, and in irate tones she hurled what apparently in her mind was the ultimate insult: she accused them of not being Freudian. Freud himself, of course, took psychoanalysis more seriously, and avoided making a game of it by saying that he himself was not a Freudian.

Recently unmasked is a new variant of 'Psychiatry' called 'Tell Me This', somewhat similar to the party pastime 'Twenty Questions'. White relates a dream or an incident, and the other members, often including the therapist, then attempt to interpret it by asking pertinent questions. As long as White answers the questions, each member continues his inquiries until he finds a question White cannot answer. Then Black sits back with a knowing look which says: 'Aha! If you could answer *that* one, you would certainly get better, so I have done *my* part.' (This is a distant relative of 'Why Don't You – Yes But'.) Some therapy groups are based almost entirely on this game, and may go on for years with only minimal change or progress. 'Tell Me This' allows much latitude to White (the patient) who, for example, can play along with it by feeling ineffectual; or he can counter it by answering all the questions offered, in which case the anger and dismay of the other players soon becomes manifest, since he is throwing back at them, 'I've answered all your questions and you haven't cured me, so what does that make you?'

'Tell Me This' is also played in schoolrooms, where the pupils know that the 'right' answer to an open-ended question asked by a certain type of teacher is not to be found by processing the factual data, but by guessing or outguessing which of several possible answers will make the teacher happy. A pedantic variant occurs in teaching ancient Greek; the teacher always has the upper hand over the pupil, and can make him look stupid and prove it in print by pointing to some obscure feature of the text. This is also often played in teaching Hebrew.

6 · STUPID

Thesis. In its milder form, the thesis of 'Stupid' is, 'I laugh with you at my own clumsiness and stupidity.' Seriously disturbed people, however, may play it in a sullen way which says, 'I am stupid, that's the way I am, so do me something.' Both forms are played from a depressive position. 'Stupid' must be distinguished from 'Schlemiel', where the position is more aggressive, and the clumsiness is a bid for forgiveness. It must also be distinguished from 'Clown', which is not a game but a pastime which reinforces the position 'I am cute and harmless.' The critical transaction in 'Stupid' is for White to make Black call him stupid or respond as though he were stupid. Hence White acts like a Schlemiel but does not ask for forgiveness; in fact forgiveness makes him uneasy, because it threatens his position. Or he behaves clownishly, but with no implication that he is kidding; he wants his behaviour to be taken seriously, as evidence of real stupidity. There is considerable external gain, since the less White learns, the more effectively he can play. Hence at school he need not study, and at work he need not go out of his way to learn anything that might lead to advancement. He has known from an early age that everyone will be satisfied with him as long as he is stupid, despite any expressions to the contrary. People are surprised when in time of stress, if he decides to come through, it turns out that he is not stupid at all – any more than is the 'stupid' younger son in the fairy tale.

Antithesis. The antithesis of the milder form is simple. By not playing, by not laughing at the clumsiness or railing at the stupidity, the anti-'Stupid' player will make a friend for life. One of the subtleties is that this game is often played by cyclothymic or manic-depressive personalities. When such people are euphoric, it seems as though they really want their associates to join in their laughter at themselves. It is often hard not to, for they give the impression that they will resent an abstainer – which in a way they do, since he threatens their position and spoils the game. But when they are depressed, and their resentment against those who laughed with or at them comes into the open, the abstainer knows that he has acted correctly. He may be the only one the patient is willing to have in the room or talk to when he is withdrawn, and all the former 'friends' who enjoyed the game are now treated as enemies.

It is no use telling White that he is not really stupid. He may actually be of quite limited intelligence and well aware of it, which is how the game got started in the first place. There may be special areas, however, in which he is superior: often psychological insight is one. It does no harm to show whatever respect is deserved for such aptitudes, but this is different from clumsy attempts at 'reassurance'. The latter may give him the bitter satisfaction of realizing that other people are even more stupid than he, but this is small consolation. Such 'reassurance' is certainly not the most intelligent therapeutic procedure; usually it is a move in a game of 'I'm Only Trying to Help You'. The antithesis of 'Stupid' is not to substitute another game, but simply to refrain from playing 'Stupid'.

The antithesis of the sullen form is a more complicated problem, because the sullen player is trying to provoke not laughter or derision but helplessness or exasperation, which he is well equipped to handle in accordance with his challenge. 'So do me something.' Thus he wins either way. If Black does nothing, it is because he feels helpless, and if he does something, it is because he is exasperated. Hence these people are prone also to play 'Why Don't You – Yes But', from which they can get the same satisfactions in milder form. There is no easy solution in this case, nor is there likely to be one forthcoming until the psychodynamics of this game are more clearly understood.

7 · WOODEN LEG

Thesis. The most dramatic form of 'Wooden Leg' is 'The Plea of Insanity'. This may be translated into transactional terms as follows: 'What do you expect of someone as emotionally disturbed as I am – that I would refrain from killing people?' To which the jury is asked to reply: 'Certainly not, we would hardly impose that restriction on you!' The 'Plea of Insanity', played as a legal game, is acceptable to American culture and is different from the almost universally respected principle that an individual may be suffering from a psychosis so profound that no reasonable person would expect him to be responsible for his actions. In Japan drunkenness, and in Russia war-time military service, are accepted as excuses for evading responsibility for all kinds of outrageous behaviour (according to this writer's information).

The thesis of 'Wooden Leg' is, 'What do you expect of a man with a wooden leg?' Put that way, of course, no one would expect anything of a man with a wooden leg except that he should steer his own wheel chair. On the other hand, during World War II there was a man with a wooden leg who used to give demonstrations of jitterbug dancing, and very competent jitterbug dancing, at Army Hospital amputation centres. There are blind men who practice law and hold political offices (one such is currently mayor of the writer's home town), deaf men who practise psychiatry and handless men who can use a typewriter.

As long as someone with a real, exaggerated or even imaginary disability is content with his lot, perhaps no one should interfere. But the moment he presents himself for psychiatric treatment, the question arises if he is using his life to his own best advantage, and if he can rise above his disability. In this country the therapist will be working in opposition to a large mass of educated public opinion. Even the close relatives of the patient who complained most loudly about the inconveniences caused by his infirmity, may eventually turn on the therapist if the patient makes definitive progress. This is readily understandable to a game analyst, but it makes his task no less difficult. All the people who were playing

'I'm Only Trying to Help You' are threatened by the impending disruption of the game if the patient shows signs of striking out on his own, and sometimes they use almost incredible measures to terminate the treatment.

Both sides are illustrated by the case of the stuttering client of Miss Black's, mentioned in the discussion of the game 'Indigence'. This man played a classical form of 'Wooden Leg'. He was unable to find employment, which he correctly attributed to the fact that he was a stutterer, since the only career that interested him, he said, was that of salesman. As a free citizen he had a right to seek employment in whatever field he chose, but as a stutterer, his choice raised some question as to the purity of his motives. The reaction of the helpful agency when Miss Black attempted to break up this game was very unfavourable to her.

'Wooden Leg' is especially pernicious in clinical practice, because the patient may find a therapist who plays the same game with the same plea, so that progress is impossible. This is relatively easy to arrange in the case of the 'Ideological Plea', 'What do you expect of a man who lives in a society like ours?' One patient combined this with the 'Psychosomatic Plea', 'What do you expect of a man with psychosomatic symptoms?' He found a succession of therapists who would accept one plea but not the other, so that none of them either made him feel comfortable in his current position by accepting both pleas, or budged him from it by rejecting both. Thus he proved that psychiatry couldn't help people.

Some of the pleas which patients use to excuse symptomatic behaviour are colds, head injuries, situational stress, the stress of modern living, American culture and the economic system. A literate player has no difficulty in finding authorities to support him. 'I drink because I'm Irish.' 'This wouldn't happen if I lived in Russia or Tahiti.' The fact is that patients in mental hospitals in Russia and Tahiti are very similar to those in American state hospitals.[1] Special pleas of 'If It Weren't For Them' or 'They Let Me Down' should always be evaluated very carefully in clinical practice – and also in social research projects.

Slightly more sophisticated are such pleas as: What do you expect of a man who (a) comes from a broken home; (b) is neurotic; (c) is in analysis or (d) is suffering from a disease known as alcoholism? These are topped by, 'If I stop doing this I won't be able to analyse it, and then I'll never get better.'

The obverse of 'Wooden Leg' is 'Rickshaw', with the thesis, 'If they only had (rickshaws) (duckbill platypuses) (girls who spoke ancient Egyptian) around this town, I never would have got into this mess.'

Antithesis. Anti-'Wooden Leg' is not difficult if the therapist can distinguish clearly between his own Parent and Adult, and if the therapeutic aim is explicitly understood by both parties.

On the Parental side, he can be either a 'good' Parent or a 'harsh' one. As a 'good' Parent he can accept the patient's plea, especially if it fits in with his own viewpoints, perhaps with the rationalization that people are not responsible for their actions until they have completed their therapy. As a 'harsh' Parent he can reject the plea and engage in a contest of wills with the patient. Both of these attitudes are already familiar to the 'Wooden Leg' player, and he knows how to extract the maximum satisfactions from each of them.

As an Adult, the therapist declines both of these opportunities. When the patient asks, 'What do you expect of a neurotic?' (or whatever plea he is using at the moment) the reply is, 'I don't expect anything. The question is, what do you expect of yourself?' The only demand he makes is that the patient give a serious answer to this question, and the only concession he makes is to allow the patient a reasonable length of time to answer it: anywhere from six weeks to six months, depending on the relationship between them and the patient's previous preparation.

REFERENCE

1. Berne, E., 'The Cultural Problem: Psychopathology in Tahiti', *American Journal of Psychiatry*, 116: 1076–1081, 1960.

12 · Good Games

THE psychiatrist, who is in the best and perhaps the only position to study games adequately, unfortunately deals almost entirely with people whose games have led them into difficulties. This means that the games which are offered for clinical investigation are all in some sense 'bad' ones. And since by definition games are based on ulterior transactions, they must all have some element of exploitation. For these two reasons, practical on the one hand and theoretical on the other, the search for 'good' games becomes a difficult quest. A 'good' game might be described as one whose social contribution outweighs the complexity of its motivations, particularly if the player has come to terms with those motivations without futility or cynicism. That is, a 'good' game would be one which contributes both to the well-being of the other players and to the unfolding of the one who is 'it'. Since even under the best forms of social action and organization a large proportion of time has to be spent in playing games, the search for 'good' ones must be assiduously pursued. Several examples are offered here, but they are admittedly deficient in both number and quality. They include 'Busman's Holiday', 'Cavalier', 'Happy to Help', 'Homely Sage' and 'They'll Be Glad They Knew Me'.

1 · BUSMAN'S HOLIDAY

Thesis. Strictly speaking, this is a pastime rather than a game, and evidently a constructive one for all concerned. An American mail carrier who goes to Tokyo to help a Japanese postman on his rounds, or an American ear-nose-and-throat specialist who spends his holiday working in a Haitian hospital, will very likely feel just as refreshed and have just as good stories to tell as if he had gone lion hunting in Africa or spent the time driving through transcontinental highway traffic. The Peace Corps has now given official sanction to Busman's Holiday.

'Busman's Holiday' becomes a game, however, if the work is secondary to some ulterior motive and is undertaken merely as a show in order to accomplish something else. Even under those circumstances, however, it still keeps its constructive quality and is one of the more commendable covers for other activities (which may also be constructive).

2 · CAVALIER

Thesis. This is a game played by men who are not under sexual pressure – occasionally by younger men who have a satisfactory marriage or liaison, more often by older men who are gracefully resigned to monogamy or celibacy. Upon encountering a suitable female subject, White takes every opportunity to remark upon her good qualities, never transgressing the limits appropriate to her station in life, the immediate social situation and the requirements of good taste. But within those limits he allows full play to his creativity, enthusiasm and originality. The object is not to seduce but to exhibit his virtuosity in the art of effective compliment. The internal social advantage lies in the pleasure given to the woman by this innocent artistry, and by her responsive appreciation of White's skill. In suitable cases, where both are aware of the nature of the game, it may be stretched with increasing delight on both sides, to the point of extravagance. A man of the world, of course, will know when to stop, and will not continue beyond the point at which he ceases to amuse (out of consideration for her) or where the quality of his offerings begins to deteriorate (out of consideration for his own pride of craftsmanship). 'Cavalier' is played for its external social advantages in the case of poets, who are as much, or more, interested in the appreciation of qualified critics and the public at large as they are in the response of the lady who inspired them.

The Europeans in romance, and the British in poetry, seem always to have been more adept at this game than the Americans. In our country it has fallen largely into the hands of the Fruit Stand school of poetry: your eyes are like avocados, your lips like cucumbers, etc. 'Cavalier', Fruit Stand Type, can hardly compare in elegance with the productions of Herrick and Lovelace, or even with the cynical but imaginative works of Rochester, Roscommon and Dorset.

Antithesis. It takes some sophistication for the woman to play her part well, and a great deal of sulkiness or stupidity for her to refuse to play it at all. The proper complement is a variant of 'Gee You're Wonderful Mr Murgatroyd' (GYWM): namely, 'I Admire Your Productions, Mr M'. If the woman is mechanical or unperceptive, she may respond with plain GYWM, but that misses the point: what White is offering for appreciation is not himself, but his poetry. The brutal antithesis from a sulky woman is to play Second-Degree 'Rapo' ('Buzz Off, Buster'). Third-Degree 'Rapo', which could conceivably occur, would of course be an unspeakably vile response under the circumstances. If the woman is merely stupid, she will play First-Degree 'Rapo', taking the compliments to feed her vanity and neglecting to appreciate White's creative efforts and abilities. In general, the game is spoiled if the woman treats it as an attempt at seduction rather than as a literary exhibition.

Relatives. 'Cavalier' being a game, it must be distinguished from the operations and procedures carried on during a straightforward courtship, which are simple transactions without ulterior motive. The female counterpart of 'Cavalier' may be conveniently called 'Blarney', since it is often played by gallant Irish ladies in their sunset years.

PARTIAL ANALYSIS

Aim: Mutual admiration.

Roles: Poet, Appreciative subject.

Social Paradigm: Adult-Adult.

  Adult (male): 'See how good I can make you feel.'

  Adult (female): 'My, but you make me feel good.'

Psychological Paradigm:

  Child (male): 'See what phrases I can create.'

  Child (female): 'My, but you're creative.'

Advantages: (1) Internal Psychological – creativity and reassurance of attractiveness. (2) External Psychological – avoids rejection for unnecessary sexual advances. (3) Internal Social – 'Cavalier'. (4) External Social – these may be resigned. (5) Biological – mutual stroking. (6) Existential – I can live gracefully.

3 · HAPPY TO HELP

Thesis. White is consistently helpful to other people, with some ulterior motive. He may be doing penance for past wickedness, covering up for present wickedness, making friends in order to exploit them later or seeking prestige. But whoever questions his motives must also give him credit for his actions. After all, people can cover up for past wickedness by becoming more wicked, exploit people by fear rather than generosity and seek prestige for evil ways instead of good ones. Some philanthropists are more interested in competition than in benevolence: 'I gave more money (works of art, acres of land) than you did.' Again, if their motives are questioned, they must nevertheless be given credit for competing in a constructive way, since there are so many people who compete destructively. Most people (or peoples) who play 'Happy to Help' have both friends and enemies, both perhaps justified in their feelings. Their enemies attack their motives and minimize their actions, while their friends are grateful for their actions and minimize their motives. Therefore so-called 'objective' discussions of this game are practically nonexistent. People who claim to be neutral soon show which side they are neutral on.

This game, as an exploitative manoeuvre, is the basis for a large proportion of 'public relations' in America. But the customers are glad to become involved, and it is perhaps the most pleasant and constructive of the commercial games. In another connection, one of its most reprehensible forms is a three-handed family game in which the mother and father compete for the affection of their offspring. But even here, it should be noted, the choice of 'Happy to Help' removes some of the discredit, since there are so many unpleasant ways of competing available – for example, 'Mummy is sicker than daddy,' or 'Why do you love him more than you love me?'

4 · HOMELY SAGE

Thesis. This is properly a script rather than a game, but it has gamelike aspects. A well-educated and sophisticated man learns as much as he can about all sorts of things besides his own business. When he reaches retirement age, he moves from the big city where he held a responsible position to a small town. There it soon becomes known that people can go to him with their problems of whatever kind, from a knock in the engine to a senile relative, and that he will help them himself if he is competent or else refer them to qualified experts. Thus he soon finds his place in his new environment as a 'Homely Sage', making no pretences, but always willing to listen. In its best form it is played by people who have taken the trouble to go to a psychiatrist to examine their motives, and to learn what errors to avoid before setting themselves up in this role.

5 · THEY'LL BE GLAD THEY KNEW ME

Thesis. This is a more worthy variant of 'I'll Show Them'. There are two forms of 'I'll Show Them'. In the destructive form White 'shows them' by inflicting damage on them. Thus he may manoeuvre himself into a superior position, not for the prestige or the material rewards but because it gives him power to exercise his spite. In the constructive form White works hard and exerts every effort to gain prestige, not for the sake of craftsmanship or legitimate accomplishment (although those may play a secondary role), nor to inflict direct damage on his enemies, but so that they will be eaten with envy and with regret for not having treated him better.

In 'They'll Be Glad They Knew Me', White is working not against but for the interests of his former associates. He wants to show them that they were justified in treating him with friendliness and respect and to demonstrate to them, for their own gratification, that their judgement was sound. In order for him to have a secure win in this game, his means as well as his ends must be honourable, and that is its superiority over 'I'll Show Them'. Both 'I'll Show Them' and 'They'll Be Glad' can be merely secondary advantages of success, rather than games. They become games when White is more interested in the effects on his enemies or friends than he is in the success itself.

PART THREE

BEYOND GAMES

13 · The Significance of Games

1. GAMES are passed on from generation to generation. The favoured game of any individual can be traced back to his parents and grandparents, and forward to his children; they in turn, unless there is a successful intervention, will teach them to his grandchildren. Thus game analysis takes place in a grand historical matrix, demonstrably extending back as far as one hundred years and reliably projected into the future for at least fifty years. Breaking this chain which involves five or more generations may have geometrically progressive effects. There are many living individuals who have more than two hundred descendants. Games may be diluted or altered from one generation to another, but there seems to be a strong tendency to inbreed with people who play a game of the same family, if not of the same genus. That is the *historical* significance of games.

2. 'Raising' children is primarily a matter of teaching them what games to play. Different cultures and different social classes favour different types of games, and various tribes and families favour different variations of these. That is the *cultural* significance of games.

3. Games are sandwiched, as it were, between pastimes and intimacy. Pastimes grow boring with repetition, as do promotional cocktail parties. Intimacy requires stringent circumspection, and is discriminated against by Parent, Adult and Child. Society frowns upon candidness, except in privacy; good sense knows that it can always be abused; and the Child fears it because of the unmasking which it involves. Hence in order to get away from the ennui of pastimes without exposing themselves to the dangers of intimacy, most people compromise for games when they are available, and these fill the major part of the more interesting hours of social intercourse. That is the *social* significance of games.

4. People pick as friends, associates and intimates other people who play the same games. Hence 'everybody who is anybody' in a given social circle (aristocracy, juvenile gang, social club, college campus, etc.) behaves in a way which may seem quite foreign to members of a different social circle. Conversely, any member of a

social circle who changes his games will tend to be extruded, but he will find himself welcome at some other social circle. That is the *personal* significance of games.

NOTE

The reader should now be in a position to appreciate the basic difference between mathematical and transactional game analysis. Mathematical game analysis postulates players who are completely rational. Transactional game analysis deals with games which are un-rational, or even irrational, and hence more real.

14 · The Players

MANY games are played most intensely by disturbed people; generally speaking, the more disturbed they are, the harder they play. Curiously enough, however, some schizophrenics seem to refuse to play games, and demand candidness from the beginning. In everyday life games are played with the greatest conviction by two classes of individuals: the Sulks, and the Jerks or Squares.

The Sulk is a man who is angry at his mother. On investigation it emerges that he has been angry at her since early childhood. He often has good 'Child' reasons for his anger: she may have 'deserted' him during a critical period in his boyhood by getting sick and going to the hospital, or she may have given birth to too many siblings. Sometimes the desertion is more deliberate; she may have farmed him out in order to remarry. In any case, he has been sulking ever since. He does not like women, although he may be a Don Juan. Since sulking is deliberate at its inception, the decision to sulk can be reversed at any period of life, just as it can be during childhood when it comes time for dinner. The requirements for reversing the decision are the same for the grown-up Sulk as for the little boy. He must be able to save face, and he must be offered something worthwhile in exchange for the privilege of sulking. Sometimes a game of 'Psychiatry' which might otherwise last several years can be aborted by reversing a decision to sulk. This requires careful preparation of the patient and proper timing and approach. Clumsiness or bullying on the part of the therapist will have no better result than it does with a sulky little boy; in the long run, the patient will pay the therapist back for his mishandling just as the little boy will eventually repay clumsy parents.

With female Sulks the situation is the same, *mutatis mutandis*, if they are angry at father. Their Wooden Leg ('What do you expect of a woman who had a father like that?') must be handled with even more diplomacy by a male therapist. Otherwise he risks being thrown into the wastebasket of 'men who are like father'.

There is a bit of Jerk in everyone, but the object of game analysis is to keep it at a minimum. A Jerk is someone who is overly sensitive to Parental influences. Hence his Adult data processing and his Child's spontaneity are likely to be interfered with at critical moments, resulting in inappropriate or clumsy behaviour. In extreme cases the Jerk merges with the Toady, the Show-off, and the Cling. The Jerk is not to be confused with the bewildered schizophrenic, who has no functioning Parent and very little functioning Adult, so that he has to cope with the world in the ego state of a confused Child. It is interesting that in common usage 'jerk' is an epithet applied to men only, or in rare cases to masculine women. A Prig is even more of a Square than a Jerk; Prig is a word usually reserved for women, but occasionally it is said of men of somewhat feminine tendencies.

15 · A Paradigm

CONSIDER the following exchange between a patient (P) and a therapist (T):

P. 'I have a new project – being on time.'

T. 'I'll try to cooperate.'

P. 'I don't care about you. I'm doing it for myself. . . . Guess what grade I got on my history test!'

T. 'B+.'

P. 'How did you know?'

T. 'Because you're afraid to get an A.'

P. 'Yes, I had an A, and I went over my paper and crossed out three correct answers and put in three wrong ones.'

T. 'I like this conversation. It's Jerk-free.'

P. 'You know, last night I was thinking how much progress I've made. I figured I was only 17 per cent Jerk now.'

T. 'Well, so far this morning it's zero, so you're entitled to 34 per cent discount on the next round.'

P. 'It all began six months ago, that time I was looking at my coffeepot and for the first time I really saw it. And you know how it is now, how I hear the birds sing, and I look at people and they're really there as people, and best of all, I'm really there. And I'm not only there, but right now I'm here. The other day I was standing in the art gallery looking at a picture, and a man came up and said, "Gauguin is very nice, isn't he?" So I said: "I like you too." So we went out and had a drink and he's a very nice guy.'

This is presented as a Jerk-free, game-free conversation between two autonomous Adults, with the following annotations:

'I have a new project – being on time.' This announcement was made after the fact. The patient was nearly always late. This time she wasn't. If punctuality had been a resolution, an act of 'will power', an imposition of the Parent on the Child, made only to be broken, it would have been announced before the fact: 'This is the last time I'll be late.' That would have been an attempt to set up a game. Her announcement was not. It was an Adult decision, a project, not a resolution. The patient continued to be punctual.

'I'll try to cooperate.' This was not a 'supportive' statement, nor the first move in a new game of 'I'm Only Trying to Help You.' The patient's hour came after the therapist's coffee break. Since she was habitually late, he had fallen into the habit of taking his time and getting back late himself. When she made her declaration, he knew she meant it, and made his. The transaction was an Adult contract which both of them kept, and not a Child teasing a Parental figure who because of his position felt forced to be a 'good daddy' and say he would cooperate.

'I don't care about you.' This emphasizes that her punctuality is a decision, and not a resolution to be exploited as part of a pseudo-compliant game.

'Guess what grade I got.' This is a pastime which both were aware of and felt free to indulge in. There was no need for him to demonstrate how alert he was by telling her it was a pastime, something she already knew, and there was no need for her to refrain from playing it just because it was called a pastime.

'B+.' The therapist reckoned that in her case this was the only possible grade, and there was no reason not to say so. False modesty or a fear of being wrong might have led him to pretend that he did not know.

'How did you know?' This was an Adult question, not a game of 'Gee You're Wonderful', and it deserved a pertinent answer.

'Yes, I had an A.' This was the real test. The patient did not sulk with rationalizations or pleas, but faced her Child squarely.

'I like this conversation.' This and the following semi-facetious remarks were expressions of mutual Adult respect, with perhaps a little Parent-Child pastime, which again was optional with both of them, and of which they were both aware.

'For the first time I really saw it.' She is now entitled to her own kind of awareness and is no longer obliged to see coffeepots and people the way her parents told her to. 'Right now I'm here.' She no longer lives in the future or the past, but can discuss them briefly if it serves a useful purpose.

'I said: "I like you too."' She is not obliged to waste time playing 'Art Gallery' with the newcomer, although she could if she chose to.

The therapist, on his part, does not feel obliged to play 'Psychiatry'. There were several opportunities to bring up questions of defence, transference and symbolic interpretation, but he was able to let these go by without feeling any anxiety. It did seem worthwhile, however, to ascertain for future reference which answers she crossed out on her examination. During the rest of the hour, unfortunately, the 17 per cent of Jerk left in the patient and the 18 per cent left in the therapist showed from time to time. In summary, the proceedings given constitute an activity enlightened with some pastime.

16 · Autonomy

THE attainment of autonomy is manifested by the release or recovery of three capacities: awareness, spontaneity and intimacy.

Awareness. Awareness means the capacity to see a coffeepot and hear the birds sing in one's own way, and not the way one was taught. It may be assumed on good grounds that seeing and hearing have a different quality for infants than for grownups,[1] and that they are more aesthetic and less intellectual in the first years of life. A little boy sees and hears birds with delight. Then the 'good father' comes along and feels he should 'share' the experience and help his son 'develop'. He says: 'That's a jay, and this is a sparrow.' The moment the little boy is concerned with which is a jay and which is a sparrow, he can no longer see the birds or hear them sing. He has to see and hear them the way his father wants him to. Father has good reasons on his side, since few people can afford to go through life listening to the birds sing, and the sooner the little boy starts his 'education' the better. Maybe he will be an ornithologist when he grows up. A few people, however, can still see and hear in the old way. But most of the members of the human race have lost the capacity to be painters, poets or musicians, and are not left the option of seeing and hearing directly even if they can afford to; they must get it secondhand. The recovery of this ability is called here 'awareness'. Physiologically awareness is eidetic perception, allied to eidetic imagery.[2] Perhaps there is also eidetic perception, at least in certain individuals, in the spheres of taste, smell and kinesthesia, giving us the artists in those fields: chefs, perfumers and dancers, whose eternal problem is to find audiences capable of appreciating their products.

Awareness requires living in the here and now, and not in the elsewhere, the past or the future. A good illustration of possibilities in American life, is driving to work in the morning in a hurry. The decisive question is: 'Where is the mind when the body is here? and there are three common cases.

1. The man whose chief preoccupation is being on time is the one who is furthest out. With his body at the wheel of his car, his mind is at the door of his office, and he is oblivious to his immediate

surroundings except insofar as they are obstacles to the moment when his soma will catch up with his psyche. This is the Jerk, whose chief concern is how it will look to the boss. If he is late, he will take pains to arrive out of breath. The compliant Child is in command, and his game is 'Look How Hard I've Tried'. While he is driving, he is almost completely lacking in autonomy, and as a human being he is in essence more dead than alive. It is quite possible that this is the most favourable condition for the development of hypertension or coronary disease.

2. The Sulk, on the other hand, is not so much concerned with arriving on time as in collecting excuses for being late. Mishaps, badly timed lights and poor driving or stupidity on the part of others fit well into his scheme and are secretly welcomed as contributions to his rebellious Child or righteous Parent game of 'Look What They Made Me Do'. He, too, is oblivious to his surroundings except as they subscribe to his game, so that he is only half alive. His body is in his car, but his mind is out searching for blemishes and injustices.

3. Less common is the 'natural driver', the man to whom driving a car is a congenial science and art. As he makes his way swiftly and skilfully through the traffic, he is at one with his vehicle. He, too, is oblivious of his surroundings except as they offer scope for the craftsmanship which is its own reward, but he is very much aware of himself and the machine which he controls so well, and to that extent he is alive. Such driving is formally an Adult pastime from which his Child and Parent may also derive satisfaction.

4. The fourth case is the person who is aware, and who will not hurry because he is living in the present moment with the environment which is here: the sky and the trees as well as the feeling of motion. To hurry is to neglect that environment and to be conscious only of something that is still out of sight down the road, or of mere obstacles, or solely of oneself. A Chinese man started to get into a local subway train, when his Caucasian companion pointed out that they could save twenty minutes by taking an express, which they did. When they got off at Central Park, the Chinese man sat down on a bench, much to his friend's surprise. 'Well,' explained the former, 'since we saved twenty minutes, we can afford to sit here that long and enjoy our surroundings.'

The aware person is alive because he knows how he feels, where he is and when it is. He knows that after he dies the trees will still be there, but he will not be there to look at them again, so he wants to see them now with as much poignancy as possible.

Spontaneity. Spontaneity means option, the freedom to choose and express one's feelings from the assortment available (Parent feelings, Adult feelings and Child feelings). It means liberation, liberation from the compulsion to play games and have only the feelings one was taught to have.

Intimacy. Intimacy means the spontaneous, game-free candidness of an aware person, the liberation of the eidetically perceptive, uncorrupted Child in all its naïveté living in the here and now. It can be shown experimentally[3] that eidetic perception evokes affection, and that candidness mobilizes positive feelings, so that there is even such a thing as 'one-sided intimacy' – a phenomenon well known, although not by that name, to professional seducers, who are able to capture their partners without becoming involved themselves. This they do by encouraging the other person to look at them directly and to talk freely, while the male or female seducer makes only a well-guarded pretence of reciprocating.

Because intimacy is essentially a function of the natural Child (although expressed in a matrix of psychological and social complications), it tends to turn out well if not disturbed by the intervention of games. Usually the adaptation to Parental influences is what spoils it, and most unfortunately this is almost a universal occurrence. But before, unless and until they are corrupted, most infants seem to be loving,[4] and that is the essential nature of intimacy, as shown experimentally.

REFERENCES

1. Berne, E., 'Intuition IV: Primal Images & Primal Judgments', *Psychiatric Quarterly*, 29: 634–658, 1955.

2. Jaensch, E. R., *Eidetic Imagery*, Harcourt, Brace, New York, 1930.

3. These experiments are still in the pilot stage at the San Francisco Social Psychiatry Seminars. The effective experimental use of transactional analysis requires special training and experience, just as the effective experimental use of chromatography or infra-red spectrophotometry does. Distinguishing a game from a pastime is no easier than distinguishing a star from a planet. See Berne, E., 'The Intimacy Experiment', *Transactional Analysis Bulletin*, 3: 113, 1964; 'More About Intimacy', ibid., 3: 125, 1964.

4. Some infants are corrupted or starved very early (marasmus, some colics) and never have a chance to exercise this capacity.

17 · The Attainment of Autonomy

PARENTS, deliberately or unaware, teach their children from birth how to behave, think, feel and perceive. Liberation from these influences is no easy matter, since they are deeply ingrained and are necessary during the first two or three decades of life for biological and social survival. Indeed, such liberation is only possible at all because the individual starts off in an autonomous state, that is, capable of awareness, spontaneity and intimacy, and he has some discretion as to which parts of his parents' teachings he will accept. At certain specific moments early in life he decides how he is going to adapt to them. It is because his adaptation is in the nature of a series of decisions that it can be undone, since decisions are reversible under favourable circumstances.

The attainment of autonomy, then, consists of the overthrow of all those irrelevancies discussed in Chapters 13, 14 and 15. And such overthrow is never final: there is a continual battle against sinking back into the old ways.

First, as discussed in Chapter 13, the weight of a whole tribal or family historical tradition has to be lifted, as in the case of Margaret Mead's villagers in New Guinea;[1] then the influence of the individual parental, social and cultural background has to be thrown off. The same must be done with the demands of contemporary society at large, and finally the advantages derived from one's immediate social circle have to be partly or wholly sacrificed. Then all the easy indulgences and rewards of being a Sulk or a Jerk, as described in Chapter 14, have to be given up. Following this, the individual must attain personal and social control, so that all the classes of behaviour described in the Appendix, except perhaps dreams, become free choices subject only to his will. He is then ready for game-free relationships such as that illustrated in the paradigm in Chapter 15. At this point he may be able to develop his capacities for autonomy. In essence, this whole preparation consists of obtaining a friendly divorce from one's parents (and from other Parental influences) so that they may be agreeably visited on occasion, but are no longer dominant.

REFERENCE

1. Mead, M., *New Lives for Old,* Gollancz, 1956.

18 · After Games, What?

THE sombre picture presented in Parts I and II of this book, in which human life is mainly a process of filling in time until the arrival of death, or Santa Claus, with very little choice, if any, of what kind of business one is going to transact during the long wait, is a commonplace but not the final answer. For certain fortunate people there is something which transcends all classifications of behaviour, and that is awareness; something which rises above the programming of the past, and that is spontaneity; and something that is more rewarding than games, and that is intimacy. But all three of these may be frightening and even perilous to the unprepared. Perhaps they are better off as they are, seeking their solutions in popular techniques of social action, such as 'togetherness'. This may mean that there is no hope for the human race, but there is hope for individual members of it.

Appendix
The Classification of Behaviour

AT any given moment a human being is engaged in one or more of the following classes of behaviour:

CLASS I. Internally programmed (archaeopsychic). Autistic behaviour.

    Orders: (*a*) Dreams.
           (*b*) Fantasies.
                Families: i. Extraneous fantasies (wish fulfilment).
                        ii. Autistic transactions, Unadapted.
                        iii. Autistic transactions, Adapted (with neopsychic programming).
           (*c*) Fugues.
           (*d*) Delusional behaviour.
           (*e*) Involuntary actions.
                Families: i. Tics.
                        ii. Mannerisms.
                        iii. Parapraxes.
           (*f*) Others.

CLASS II. Probability programmed (neopsychic). Reality-tested behaviour.

    Orders: (*a*) Activities.
                Families: i. Professions, trades, etc.
                        ii. Sports, hobbies, etc.
           (*b*) Procedures.
                 Families: i. Data processing.
                        ii. Techniques.
           (*c*) Others.

CLASS III. Socially programmed (partly exteropsychic). Social behaviour.

    Orders: (*a*) Rituals and ceremonies.
           (*b*) Pastimes.
           (*c*) Operations and manoeuvres.
           (*d*) Games.

Suborders: A. Professional games (angular transactions).

B. Social games (duplex transactions).

(*e*) Intimacy.

In this scheme the social games previously discussed would be classified as follows: Class III, Socially programmed; Order (*d*), Games; Suborder B, Social Games

Intimacy, 'the end of the line', is the final classification, and is part of game-free living.

The reader should feel free to carp (but not to gleek or fleer) at the above classification. It is included not because the writer is in love with it, but because it is more functional, real and practical than other systems now in use and can be helpful to those who like or need taxonomy.

Index of Pastimes [P] and Games [G]

Author Index

Subject Index